A TREASURY OF ENGLISH APHORISMS

A TREASURY OF ENGLISH APHORISMS

EDITED, WITH AN INTRODUCTION, BY
LOGAN PEARSALL SMITH

LONDON
CONSTABLE AND COMPANY LTD
1947

LONDON

PUBLISHED BY

CONSTABLE AND COMPANY LTD

10—12 ORANGE STREET W C 2

·

INDIA

LONGMANS, GREEN AND COMPANY LTD

BOMBAY   CALCUTTA   MADRAS

·

CANADA

LONGMANS, GREEN AND COMPANY LTD

TORONTO

Printed in Great Britain by Butler & Tanner Ltd., Frome and London

I MUST thank Mr. Mackail, Mr. Santayana, and Mr. Bernard Shaw for permission to reprint extracts from their writings. Mrs. Creighton has permitted me to reprint some of the sentences from her life of Bishop Creighton, and has most kindly sent me a few of his unpublished sayings. The sentences from Samuel Butler are reprinted by the kind permission of Mr. Festing Jones and Messrs. Jonathan Cape, Limited; for those of Churton Collins I am indebted to Mrs. L. C. Collins and the Editor of the *English Review*. Messrs. George Allen & Unwin, Ltd., have allowed me to reprint some sentences from Bradley's *Appearance and Reality*, Messrs. Methuen & Co., Ltd., some of Oscar Wilde's aphorisms, and Mr. John Murray a few of Benjamin Jowett's sayings. For permission to reprint the extracts from Stevenson's works, and from Emerson's Journals I am indebted to Messrs. Chatto & Windus, Charles Scribner's Sons, and the Houghton Mifflin Company.

A list of the authors and books quoted, and an explanation of the references, will be found at the end of the volume.

I must thank Mr. Macleill, Mr. Santayana, and Mr. Bernard Shaw for permission to reprint extracts from their writings. Mr. Creighton has permitted me to reprint some of the sentences from some of his unpublished sayings. The sentences from Samuel Butler are reprinted by the kind permission of Mrs. Festing Jones and Messrs. A. C. Fifield; Capel Lofft's, for those of Churton Collins I am indebted to Mr. L. C. Collins and the Editor of the Saturday Review. Messrs. George Allen & Unwin Ltd. have allowed me to reprint some sentences from Thoreau's Appreciation by Bazalgette; Messrs. Methuen & Co. Ltd., some of Oscar Wilde's aphorisms; and Mr. John Murray a few of Benjamin Jowett's sayings have permission to reprint the extracts from Seventeen Lectures, and from Emerson; Jowett I am indebted to Messrs. Chatto & Windus; Charles Whibley's books and the Hogarth and Mifflin Company.

A list of the authors and books quoted, and an explanation of the references, will be found at the end of the volume.

CONTENTS

CONTENTS

A TREASURY OF ENGLISH APHORISMS

INTRODUCTION

BACON in his *Advancement of Learning* draws a distinction between two ways of writing, writing in what he calls "Method," and writing in Aphorisms. By method he means formal discourse, comprehensive surveys and chains of reasoning, and all the arts of order and arrangement which give their shape to a scientific treatise or literary composition. Writing in aphorisms, or disconnected sentences, is, on the other hand, a "broken" way of stating truth; and yet it has, Bacon adds, many advantages. Being the presentation of knowledge "in growth," aphorisms provoke further inquiry; and they are a test, moreover, of the value of the thought of those who write them; for discarding, as such writers must, all comment and illustration and elucidation, they have only the "pith and heart" of observation to rely on; aphorisms devoid of this are ridiculous: only those who are "sound and grounded" can compose them.

The method of writing in aphorisms which Bacon thus describes is a very ancient form of expression: it was familiar to the Greeks; many sentences attributed to various Greek sages and philosophers have come down to us, and classical literature is full of apophthegms and wise sayings. But the history of the aphorism goes much farther back, for it was in this form that the wisdom of the Egyptians found expression, and in old papyri are preserved a number of almost dateless saws and maxims. In the Wisdom Books of the Bible, in Ecclesiastes, in the Proverbs of Solomon, in Ecclesiasticus, we possess large collections of them; and they are found in most of the modern literatures of Europe, in Italian, in Spanish, in German. It is in France, however, that this way of writing has been most carefully cultivated, and has come to be regarded as one of the minor arts of literature—as a delicate form worthy of special interest and attention. This is due in the first place to the fame of a famous little book, the *Maximes* of La Rochefoucauld, in which the aphorism was given its consummate stamp and polish, and the perfection to which it could attain was made brilliantly apparent. Then on this masterpiece followed that astonishing book, Pascal's *Pensées*, which, though it contains much else, is full of profound and brilliant aphorisms; and the tradition thus established by these writers, and carried on by La Bruyère, by Vauvenargues, by Rivarol and Chamfort and Joubert, has enriched the literature of France with whole constellations of glittering thoughts and phrases.

It is generally supposed that we possess but a meagre store of aphorisms in English; that our language is unsuited to this mode of expression, and that few of our writers have handled it with much success. Thus Lord Morley, the only one of our critics who has written at length on the subject, has said: "The obvious truth is that in this department our literature is particularly weak, while French literature is particularly strong in it. With the exception of Bacon, we possess

2

no writer of apophthegms of the first order."[1]   This is a sweeping statement; but when we note that in his list of English aphorists Lord Morley ignores almost all our authors who have achieved success in this way of writing; that he says nothing of Halifax or Chesterfield or Blake or Hazlitt or Emerson, and hardly mentions the name of our greatest master of sententious precepts and wise sayings; and when we find that Dean Inge, in a recent essay on the subject, also overlooks these writers, we cannot but question the justice of this generally accepted opinion, and suspect that the sense of our poverty in this department of literature is due, not so much to a real indigence, as to an unawareness of the stores which we really do possess.   To examine these stores with a closer attention, to collect and put together some of their finer specimens, will be, therefore, a not unprofitable task; and such an investigation and voyage of discovery is the purpose of this book.   In these but half-explored depths we may find—I believe we shall find—a great richness of forgotten treasures—treasures, I cannot but think, equal to those of any other country—and in our English waters we shall undoubtedly witness the sporting and blowing of one great leviathan, one whale of unequalled proportions.

Before we start out, however, it will be well to define for ourselves the precise object of our search. What exactly is the aphorism, by what marks shall we know it when we find it, of what substance is it composed, and what is the form of its composition?   What are the advantages and what the drawbacks and limitations of this way of expression?   The word "aphorism," meaning literally a definition or distinction, is

[1] John Morley, *Critical Miscellanies*, 1886, Vol. II, p. 20.

of medical origin; it was first used of the Aphorisms of Hippocrates, the father of medicine as he is called. Writing in aphorisms, or brief, disconnected sentences, is often made use of in the early stages of a science like medicine, where the acquired knowledge, being the disconnected record of empirical facts, cannot be treated or set forth in any systematic fashion. Hippocrates begins his collection of medical aphorisms with one of the most famous of all famous sayings, with the sentence, "Art is long, life is short"; but already, before his date, Heraclitus had made use of this form of statement to express truths about life of a wide import—"Character is destiny," for instance; "We cannot step twice into the same river"; "The waking have one and the same world, but the sleeping have each a world of their own." The word "aphorism" has come to denote any brief, sententious statement, "any principle or precept expressed in a few words," as the Oxford Dictionary defines it, "a short pithy statement containing a truth of general import." It is distinguished from the axiom, which is the statement of a self-evident truth, and also from the theorem, which is a demonstrable proposition in science and mathematics. The theorem that "the three angles of a triangle are equal to two right angles," though the embodiment of a general truth, is not an aphorism, for the aphorism concerns itself with life and human nature, and its truths are incapable of scientific demonstration. The prose epigram, on the other hand, though concerned with life like the aphorism, and possessing its terse and pointed form, is lacking in general import;—it is not the statement of a general truth. Other words with much the same signification as aphorism, are "maxim," "apophthegm," "saying"; and although these have sometimes been distinguished from each other—the "maxim" being defined as containing not only a general truth, but also advice and admonition, and the apophthegm or saying as an aphorism or maxim expressed in speech—yet these distinctions of the rhetoricians are not of much importance, and have seldom been observed in the current usage of the words. "Sentence" and "gnome" are old names for the aphorism which have fallen out of use.

Among the aphorisms which are most familiar to us are the legal maxims which are supposed to embody certain fundamental principles of law: "The public welfare is the highest good," for instance, "The King can do no wrong," "An Englishman's house is his castle," "Ignorance of the law excuses no one,"— maxims like these have been given an authority in common law equal to that of legal enactments, and judicial decisions have been often based upon them. Aphorisms about life in general are like these axioms of jurisprudence, brief, detached, isolated observations; and like the maxim, "The King can do no wrong," they are often very partial statements of the truth They are generally printed without any very definite order or arrangement—they are collections of scraps and fragments of truth. Books like these are unsuitable for prolonged reading; what is sometimes our feeling towards them was expressed by Edward FitzGerald, when he prefaced a collection of this kind with the remark, "few books are duller than books of Aphorisms." And yet such books are not without their fascination; we throw them down, but take them up again; they are unreadable, and yet we read them; and since so many collections of aphorisms have survived through the ages and have been constantly reprinted, it is plain that this way of presenting truth must have certain merits and advantages of its own.

Experience is always seeking for special literary forms in which its various aspects can find their most adequate expression; and there are many of these aspects which are best rendered in a fragmentary fashion, because they are themselves fragments of experience, gleams and flashes of light, rather than the steady glow of a larger illumination. The disconnected impressions which we derive from life form a kind of knowledge "in growth," as Bacon called it; an over-early and peremptory attempt to digest this knowledge into a system tends, as he suggests, to falsify and distort it. Collections of disconnected truths, or half-truths, about human nature never lose their value, while the ambitious schemes which the philosophers build upon them soon collapse and are forgotten. Life, as Dr. Johnson said, "is not the object of science; we see a little, very little"; and the great psychological investigation of himself, which is man's most fascinating pursuit upon this planet, is still in that early stage when its observations are empirical and scattered. Such observations still find their most unhampered expression in those terse sentences and sayings which are the embodiment of wise principles of conduct, of central truths about the world and life and human nature. Aphorisms are no flights of fancy, no fruits culled from the Hesperian gardens of the imagination; they are products of the familiar earth, and smack of the world we live in. They cover the whole field of practical experience, from the lowest maxims of shopkeeping prudence to the highest rules of conduct; and our knowledge of ourselves and others, of the human heart and its springs of action, of love and hate and envy and ambition, of the characters and manners of mankind, of all the weaknesses and follies and absurdities of human nature, is embodied and stored up in this immense accumulation of wise observations. It is from these, rather than from any systematic treatises on human nature, we can learn with most profit what stuff we are made of, and what are the causes of success or failure in the great experiment of living.

This gnomic wisdom, it has been said, and truly said, is the true salt of literature, and those books, at least in prose, are most nourishing which are most saturated with it. Many historians and essayists have enriched their works with an abundance of aphoristic sayings; we find them in the speeches of Thucydides, in Plutarch's Lives, in the writings of Tacitus and Seneca, in the essays of Montaigne and Emerson. Though they belong more to the element of prose than that of poetry, the poets have not neglected them; they abound in the Greek drama, in the plays of Shakespeare; and the verse of Pope and his school consists largely of rhymed aphorisms and maxims.

The impulse to embody observation in durable phrases, in the happy rhythm and run of memorable words—this impulse, which has produced so large a store of proverbs in every language, is evidently a strong impulse in human nature: the aphorism is its flowering after it has been transplanted into the soil of cultivated minds. An aphorism has been defined as a proverb coined in a private mint, and the definition is a happy one; for the aphorism, like the proverb, is the result of observation, and however private and superior the mint, the coins it strikes must, to find acceptance, be made of current metal. In other words, the aphorist must draw for the most part on common experience; a main part of his task is to say in a more striking form what, in Pope's familiar words,

> Oft was thought but ne'er so well expressed.

He is a dealer, therefore, in commonplaces, and unless he is very careful his truths will turn into truisms—and what for him is the worst fate of all—into moral truisms on his hands. We are already prejudiced against him as a sententious bore; if in addition he becomes a hortatory and didactic one, with what eagerness shall we not stop our ears to his admonitions! He can only win our tolerance by making us believe that he has no moral axe to grind; that he is a detached and disinterested spectator, who is telling us the truth, and not attempting to improve us. This need to maintain at all costs the appearance of a veracious observer tends however of itself to compromise the aphorist's veracity, or to limit him at least to certain aspects of the truth. In his dread of slipping into the seas of tepid platitude which surround him on every side, he is apt to cling, almost in desperation, to the sharpest rocks of bleak reality. The more pungent and caustic his sayings, the more we like them; they are the hornets and wasps, and not the butterflies of reflection; or if they are butterflies, they are like them, gross feeders, and nourish themselves on the less ideal aspects of existence.

Men have embodied in hymns their heavenly hopes and aspirations, and in lyrics their illusions and enchanted joys; but disenchantment, the ever-accumulating stores of wise disillusion and worldly wisdom, are the aspects of life which, it would seem, the aphorism is best fitted to express. Famous aphorists are not therefore often found among the panegyrists of human nature or the eulogists of life; and although some of them have now and then attempted to speak with angels' voices (and to embody in a brief saying some spiritual or poetic truth is perhaps their greatest triumph), yet the attempt is a perilous one, and requires a genius like Blake's or Emerson's to avoid disaster. We have only to compare the attitude of the poets with that of the aphorists towards a subject like Love —what Shelley and what Dr. Johnson, for instance, say about it—to be struck by the difference in their respective points of view. Aphorisms are apt, indeed, to be somewhat fulsome if they are too sweetly flavoured; such sentences offend our taste as a cynical lyric would offend it, or an atheistic hymn; we turn from them with a kind of literary nausea to welcome as an antidote the most outrageous paradox.

And yet paradox is another pitfall for the aphorist, another dangerous lion in his path. No brief statement can indeed be absolutely true; "almost every wise saying," it has been said, "has an opposite one, equally wise, to balance it." An aphorism can present at best but one aspect of the truth, and sometimes by reversing it attention is called to some more subtle aspect—"Punctuality is the thief of time," for instance, or Oscar Wilde's dictum that "It is only shallow people who do not judge by appearances," or again the paradox of Mr. Chesterton, that lord of paradoxes, "Whatever is worth doing at all is worth doing badly." But paradoxes, however much they may amuse us at the moment, have seldom weight enough to give them enduring value. Wise sayings, to ring true, must be made of sterling metal, must embody a feeling more profound than the mere desire to flout general opinion and reverse its judgments; we soon tire of the sparkle, the glitter, the polished brass of these false coins of thought.

It is not only however the danger of platitude which has given the aphorism a cynical twist and a bitter flavour. The necessity of this form of expression, the need to be brief and sharp and pointed, tends to limit it, as has been said, to the portrayal of the obliquities and follies of human nature, which are striking and easy to depict, while its more luminous aspects are diffused and vague, and less capable of brief notation. The greatest aphorists, the most accomplished masters of this form, have been sardonic observers of their fellow human beings; and it was the most famous of them all, La Rochefoucauld, who brought into striking relief the least edifying aspects of man's nature, his all-devouring egotism and the littleness and meanness of his moral character. Pascal added to this picture a truly appalling indictment of the imbecility and impotence of the mind of man, and the general disgrace of his mortal condition. The humane and optimistic thinkers of the eighteenth century found this sinister portrait a revolting one; they were horrified to see their own faces reflected in so black a mirror. They attempted therefore to turn against these maligners of humanity their own weapons. Voltaire published an edition of Pascal's *Pensées* with terse and witty comments, and his friend Vauvenargues tried to restore by aphorisms what La Rochefoucauld's aphorisms had so seriously damaged—man's belief in the nobility of his own nature. Vauvenargues' spirit was a lofty one; Lord Morley is no doubt right when he tells us that he and other thinkers of his kind have chosen the nobler part. His famous saying, "Great thoughts come from

the heart," may be truer, as it is certainly more uplift-
ing, than a maxim of La Rochefoucauld which unmasks
our selfishness and vanity; it has however one drawback—it is not nearly so good an aphorism. Vauvenargues is the nobler soul, but the sardonic duke—and
the point is not without importance—is more finely
aware of what the aphorism is best fitted to express,
and of the way it can find its most perfect expression.

Human nature has suffered of late, however, many
disgraces, and the noble view of man has fallen somewhat out of fashion. Much more fully aware, as
we are, of our humble status in the universe, of our
nearer kinship to the apes than to the angels, and of
the gruesome history of our species on this planet,
we do not find ourselves greatly shocked by this old-
fashioned cynicism; nor can students of pscho-analysis
share the indignation of those Victorian critics who
declared that such thoughts "tarnish the brightness of
the soul; they degrade the heart." Yet aphorisms
like La Rochefoucauld's, although they may not shock
us—so far since his date has mankind fallen—are by
no means to the taste of all modern readers. There
are many who feel with Lord Morley—though not
perhaps for Lord Morley's reasons—that the truths
which aphorisms are apt to embody are not truths
upon which they very much care to dwell. This
wisdom of the world they find unimaginative and
earthy; it has for them a musty taste; if they are to
feast on essences, they prefer to sip the honey-dew and
milk of Paradise of the poets.

But for those who prefer a drier vintage, for whom
the spectacle of life as it is, stripped of its illusions,
possesses an inexhaustible fascination; who wish to
know the truth about themselves and their fellows—for

such students of human nature there will always be a great attraction in these profound X-rays of observation, which reveal the bones beneath the flesh; these acute and penetrating phrases which puncture man's pretentions and bring them disenflated to the earth. They find such correctives medicinable as well, like that infusion of myrrh into the festival goblet, which, as one of our old divines tells us, renders the wine of life bitter, but makes it wholesome.

Aphorisms have also a practical value of another kind. We frequently fall into error and folly, Dr. Johnson tells us, "not because the true principles of action are not known, but because, for a time, they are not remembered." To compress therefore the great and obvious rules of life into brief sentences which are not easily forgotten is, as he said, to confer a real benefit upon us.

Although aphorisms are generally an embodiment of common experience, their authors need by no means always confine themselves to the pointed expression of what other people clearly think and feel. The minds of all of us are haunted by thoughts which have not yet found expression, and it is often the happy fortune of the aphorist to drag from its obscurity some such dim intuition, or confused bit of experience; to clothe it in words and bring it into daylight for our delighted recognition. These thoughts are, as Dr. Johnson said in his famous definition of wit, both natural and new; they are not obvious, but when they are put before us, we acknowledge their justice; we have not found them ourselves, but we wonder how we could have missed them. It is an even greater triumph for the aphorist when, in a flash of insight, he can perceive, and having perceived, can express some thought or feeling that has been lying buried within us, some experience of which we have never been aware before. It is not only in the regions of self-love that, as La Rochefoucauld said, there are many lands which still await their explorers; after an investigation which has lasted for thousands of years, there are many aspects of man's moral nature of which he is still ignorant, many recesses of his heart which have never yet been sounded; and the explorer of these regions, the diver into these depths, will often find much of rare value to reward him.

The human mind, a philosopher has told us, "always celebrates a little triumph whenever it can formulate a truth"; and the measure of that triumph will depend upon the importance of the truth thus embodied in a formula of words. If we ask therefore what the aphorism is in its quintessence, and what is the quality which gives it importance and enduring value, we have only to read the sayings of some great master of life, some Pascal or Goethe, whose intuitions seem to penetrate to the very core of human experience, and whose words remain in our minds, as sparks, in the poet's phrase, "of inextinguishable thought."

To polish commonplaces and give them a new lustre; to express in a few words the obvious principles of conduct, and to give to clear thoughts an even clearer expression; to illuminate dimmer impressions and bring their faint rays to a focus; to delve beneath the surface of consciousness to new veins of precious ore, to name and discover and bring to light latent and unnamed experience; and finally to embody the central truths of life in the breadth and terseness of memorable phrases — all these are the opportunities of the aphorist; and to take advantage of these opportunities, he must be a thinker, an accurate observer, a profound moralist, a psychologist, and an artist as well. Above all an artist! So great are the difficulties of his task, so numerous are the pitfalls which beset him, so repellent the pompous attitude which his tedious, stilted and oracular mode of expression forces upon him, that it is only by the greatest care that he can escape these perils; and Lord Morley's admonition to the would-be aphorist—"beware of cultivating this delicate art"—is no doubt a sound one. For the aphorist's pills, if we are to swallow them, must be gilded pills; his coins, if they are to be added to the currency of thought, must be minted of the most precious metal; many grains must be sifted from the sands of life to compose them, many thoughts and observations melted and fused together to give them weight. Each aphorism should contain, as Hazlitt said, the essence or ground-work of a separate essay; it should be the concentration or residuum of much meditation, and it must glitter with the finest sheen; for "weight," as one of our masters of this art has expressed it—"weight without lustre is lead."

A famous French aphorist, whose life, he said, was spent in chasing these butterflies of thought, and who was cursed, he also tells us, with the ambition to put a whole book into a page, a whole page into a phrase, and that phrase into a word, has revealed to us some of the secrets of this difficult art, which his compatriots have brought to such perfection. " A finished and perfect thought," Joubert writes, "what time it takes, how rare it is, and what an immense delight!" Such a thought embodied in a few memorable words was enough of itself to make illustrous the name of its maker. Sharpness, clearness, fitness, are required for its expression, and transparency is its beauty. And yet clearness is not of itself enough, the sufficient word does not suffice; an aphorism is something more than the plain statement of a truth; it must possess the quality of style as well. Joubert distinguishes between two kinds of style, two ways of writing: there is the pictorial style, rich in light and shadow and full of images, with which the author paints, as it were, upon the page; and there is the sculptor's style, which cuts deep and gives relief and outline to the subject. This austere, almost colourless style, full of economies and rejections, is the style appropriate for these engraved medallions, these finely minted coins of thought. And finally—and this is their supreme perfection—aphorisms should bear, like coins, the personal image, delicate and delicately cut, of the lord of thought from whose mint they issue. The thought, in the other words, must be stamped with the hall-mark of the mind that thinks it. The individual quality of his temper, his imagination, the tamber of his voice, must mark his sayings as his own; we must feel that they are his, that he, and only he, could have said them.

Such then at their best are these scintillations of thought, these minute and shining masterpieces of expression. We are startled at first by their novelty; we catch our breath and gaze for a moment blankly at them. Then, as we ponder their meaning and recall our past, their truth, as well as their lucid perfection, delights us. Like shooting stars, they seem to leave a track of gold behind them; like flashes of lightning they reveal the familiar world in a sudden, strange illumination; the accompanying din alarms us, till, from far ranges of experience, echoes return in long reverberations to confirm them.

In one of his note-books Coleridge wrote, "I should like to know whether or how far the delight I feel, and have always felt, in adages and aphorisms of universal or very extensive application is a general or common feeling with men, or a peculiarity of my own mind."[1] The delight of our great English critic has apparently not been shared by his countrymen, since, as I have said, our rich store of aphorisms has been so slightly regarded. It is difficult for me, and will be difficult, I believe, for anyone who may read this book, to regard as anything but preposterous Lord Morley's statement that "with the exception of Bacon, we possess no writer of apophthegms of the first order." Bacon, however, if by no means the greatest, is at least the earliest of our English aphorists. He not only collected in his *Apophthegms* a large number of other people's sayings, and also wrote in his *de Auxiliis* many Latin maxims, but he embodied as well in his essays many saws and aphoristic sentences. His essays have been called a mosaic of aphorisms, and many sentences of this kind are to be found in his *Advancement of Learning*. In these aphorisms of Bacon we already find two characteristics which mark the English as contrasted with the French aphorism. The French aphorism is often the expression of the bitterest pessimism. Many of the sayings of La Rochefoucauld, of Pascal, and above all of Chamfort, seem to be written with sulphuric acid and to scorch the page on which we read them. Vitriolic sayings of this kind are, however, rare in English, and are replaced

[1] *Anima Poetæ*, p. 300.

by a kind of practical and prosaic wordliness which is almost more distasteful than the profoundest disillusion. Bacon's maxims are for the most part concerned with the means of personal success in courts and politics—good advice, as Blake said of them, "for Satan's kingdom," and they smack of what Bacon himself called the wisdom of rats and foxes. He is concerned with the externals of character and conduct, rather than with an analysis of the inner motives of human nature; and in his preoccupation with worldly success, he has been followed by many other English aphorists, from Halifax and Chesterfield to the prudential saws and shopkeeping maxims of Benjamin Franklin. We find also now and then in Bacon's sayings another and contrasted quality, which Sainte-Beuve, in his essay on Chesterfield, noted as a characteristic of English aphorists—an element of imagination and poetry in their wit. Although for the most part dry, jejune, sententious, Bacon's phrases flash like jewels now and then. "Revenge is a kind of Wild Justice," he writes; "Faces are but a Gallery of Pictures: and Talk but a tinkling Cymbal, where there is no Love." Bacon's sentences, however, being written before La Rochefoucauld had found for the aphorism its perfect form—before it had become the custom to polish phrases and print them by themselves—are as a rule somewhat heavy, and lack the conciseness and finish of aphorisms at their best. They possess, however, a merit which is one of the greatest merits in this way of writing, they are authentically his own. "Reading maketh a full Man; Conference a ready Man; and Writing an exact Man"; "Wives are young Men's Mistresses; Companions for middle Age; and old Men's Nurses"—these terse, pithy, familiar sayings bear the indisputable mark of the mint-master who has coined them.

The next English aphorist after Bacon is another great lawyer, John Selden, and his *Table Talk* is well known for its sound good sense, its homely English wit and humour. It is also, like Bacon's Essays, a treasure-house of worldly wisdom, and presents a very vivid picture of the habits and thought and modes of expression of a learned, hard-headed, liberal-minded, but rather scornful English lawyer. Selden, more than any English aphorist, expresses that contempt for women which is often a characteristic of this class of writers, who, since they have all been men, have naturally, as Dr. Johnson said, put the blame on women "for making the world miserable." It is right, this legal authority tells us, that a man who will have a wife should meet her bills, "for he that will keep a Monkey, 'tis fit he should pay for the glasses she breaks."

Misogyny could hardly be carried farther; but aphorisms of this unamiable class are not numerous in English, and Mrs. Poyser, our great female aphorist of fiction, answered these masculine libels on her sex with pungent adequacy, when she remarked, "I'm not denyin' the women are foolish; God Almighty made 'em to match the men."

Selden did not write his aphorisms; they are sayings noted down by his secretary from his talk. Conversation is indeed one of the main sources of the aphorist; and it is generally when minds clash in talk together that these sparks are struck out—that these witty sayings find their perfected expression. Many collections of sayings have been made from the table-talk of famous persons, of Luther, of Goethe, of Dr.

Johnson, and Coleridge; and more than one Greek or Chinese sage has by one single remark achieved immortal fame. La Rochefoucauld's maxims were polished in Madame de Sablé's salon, and some of Pascal's also; Rivarol and Chamfort were famous talkers; and Joubert's *Pensées* were largely suggested by his conversations with Fontanes and Chateaubriand, and come to us clarified by these brilliant minds and filtered through them. The wealth indeed of aphorisms in French, and their shining quality, is largely due to the supremacy in talk of that social nation, and their deliberate cultivation of the arts of human intercourse. The great flood of delightful talk which has flowed for so many centuries through the salons and palaces of France has left behind it on the shores of time a bright sediment of imperishable sayings—of shining pebbles and iridescent shells rounded and polished by those waves.

Our next great English aphorist, George Savile, Marquis of Halifax, was one of the most famous conversationalists of his age. Lord Halifax, who was born in 1633, was a great statesman, in whom was embodied that moderation, that political good sense which is John Bull's most admirable characteristic; but in whom, as his editor, Sir Walter Raleigh has said, we enjoy the rare delight of finding John Bull a wit. Lord Halifax's wit, which alarmed his contemporaries and seemed to them a fault of character, may have injured his influence in practical affairs, but we cannot but be grateful for it, as it gives a brilliant quality to his writings, and again and again it flashes out in his aphorisms. These aphorisms, which were written between 1690 and 1695, after La Rochefoucauld had started the fashion for this way of writing, but which were not published till long after Halifax's death, form the most notable collection of aphorisms which we possess in English, our nearest parallel to the French collections of this kind. Into these maxims—there are more than six hundred of them—Halifax distilled the essence of his thought and observation, his profound experience of politics and life. In his political maxims, in all he says of kings and ministers, of parliaments and mobs and parties, he tells us, as his editor has pointed out, many things which other politicians know but never say; and taking us behind the scenes, he shows us the wires which move the bedizened puppets that play their parts upon that illustrious scene.

"State-business," he tells us, "is a cruel Trade; Good nature is a Bungler in it." "It is the Fools and Knaves that make the Wheels of the World turn. *They* are *the World;* those few who have Sense or Honesty sneak up and down single, but never go in Herds." "The Government of the World is a great thing," we are assured by one who played a notable part in it; but, he adds, "a very coarse one, too, compared with the Fineness of Speculative Knowledge."

To his Political Aphorisms Halifax added a large number of "Moral Thoughts and Reflections" treating without illusion, but without malice, the stock subjects of the moral aphorist, Man and his passions, his youth and age, his knavery and self-deception and folly.

Halifax, like other authors who possess the aphoristic turn of thought and expression, often enriches with aphorisms his essays and other compositions. His *Advice to a Daughter*, written before her marriage for his daughter Elizabeth, who afterwards became the mother of another famous aphorist, the Earl of

Chesterfield, is full of wise and disillusioned sentences, which picture life as it is, and offer no great hopes of happiness. Lady Elizabeth's husband, he seems to suggest, will very likely be a spendthrift, a libertine or a drunkard; but the best she can do is to turn a blind eye to his failings, rejoicing indeed that he is not without them, "for a Husband without Faults is a dangerous Observer." As to her children, she was to have as strict a guard on herself among them, as if she were among her enemies: a wise remark, as Sir Walter Raleigh says, but not one, he adds, which makes home seem a cheerful place.

The more one reads Halifax's writings, the more one is impressed by their interest and importance. His *Character of Charles II* is a masterpiece of portraiture, equal to anything in Saint-Simon's memoirs; his *Character of a Trimmer* is full of the profoundest political wisdom, and the aphorisms scattered throughout his essays are, with his separately-printed *Thoughts and Reflections*, among the best in our own or any language. They are sometimes poetic in their expression and enriched by shining images: "There is a Smell in our Native Earth, better than all the Perfumes of the East"; "Esteem to Virtue is like a cherishing Air to Plants and Flowers, which maketh them blow and prosper"; our frailties "pull our Rage by the Sleeve, and whisper Gentleness to us in our Censures"—in phrases like these we find that imaginative quality which Sainte-Beuve noted as characteristically English.

It is, however, their subtlety of thought, their profundity of observation, more than their phrasing, which impresses most the reader of Halifax's *Thoughts and Reflections*. We note certain sayings which strike us at the first perusal; and when we read the book again, others, and still others, begin to gleam on the page and darkly shine, like little wells in whose depths some truth is half-apparent.

We are told by a contemporary that many of Lord Halifax's reflections occurred to him suddenly in conversation with his friends; we cannot but ask ourselves, however, who of his contemporaries were worthy to be the friends and intellectual companions of this spiritual son of Montaigne, who was nourished on his essays, and who appears to us a somewhat lonely figure in the gay and shallow world of the Restoration, in the politics of which, nevertheless, he played a part of such importance, although, both as a statesman and as an author, his name is barely remembered now.

The name of the next great aphorist on our list, Halifax's grandson, Lord Chesterfield, has not been obscured by Time; yet Time, by tarnishing it, has treated it with even more injustice. To be distinguished and forgotten—or rather to have one's name live on, as Halifax's has lived, in the memory of a few distinguished spirits—this is a much more kindly fate than to glare before the public in the limelight which a series of unlucky incidents has cast upon the figure of Lord Chesterfield. The most damaging, in the eyes of posterity, of these incidents, is the famous clash or encounter of this piece of delicate procelain, with one of the weightiest vessels and hugest iron pots that ever swam in English waters. Dr. Johnson's letter to the patron who had failed him, full of immoderate, barely-deserved, but immortal indignation, would suffice to sink any reputation; and another giant of our literature, Charles Dickens, has in his character, or caricature, of Sir John Chester dealt,

with almost equal force and unfairness, another
blow at this accomplished but un-English figure.
The incident, however, which most shocked Lord
Chesterfield's contemporaries was the publication
after his death of his letters to his son. The son
was illegitimate, and the letters intimate; designed
though they were for a particular character and a
special purpose—to prepare namely a shy and awkward boy, born out of wedlock, for the diplomatic
service, and teach him the good manners indispensable in that career—they were read as if they contained
everything Lord Chesterfield regarded as necessary
to form a complete system of moral education for the
young.

Few things are more shocking to those who practise the
arts of success than the frank description of those arts:
that one should practise what one preaches is generally
agreed, but anyone who has the indiscretion to preach
what both he and his hearers practise must always
incur—as Lord Chesterfield has incurred—the gravest
moral reprobation. Lord Chesterfield was a man of
the world, and avowed himself as such; like his grandfather he had played an illustrious part in public affairs,
and he had also preserved, what so few who play
such parts preserve, an uninjured reputation. His
knowledge of men and affairs, of the causes of success
and failure, were the fruit of much experience and
profound observation. As the grandfather had wished
to do for Chesterfield's mother, so the grandson, with
an impulse apparently hereditary in the family, desired
to do for his son, to impart to him the acquired knowledge of a lifetime, and supply by his own experience
the boy's ignorance of the world. This world, which
the old nobleman knew so well, the world he had

mastered and enjoyed, and which, having retired from it, he viewed with complete disillusion, was that limited but lucid world of eighteenth-century society which reached its most shining perfection in France, whence its illumination spread over the rest of Europe. Of this finished culture, this achieved civilization, this rational, epicurean mastery of the art of living, Lord Chesterfield was the most accomplished and finished representative in England. He was as much at home in Paris as he was in London; Voltaire and Montesquieu were his friends, as well as the diplomatists and great ladies of the Paris salons; he shared the rational enthusiasms of the French thinkers, as well as the cynical wisdom of France's statesmen; he was, unlike Lord Halifax, completely at home in the age in which he lived; breathing its air and basking in its golden sunshine, he enjoyed to the full the fruits which were brought to ripeness by them. Among the fairest of these fruits was a certain exquisite art of social intercourse, a delicate perfection and grace and bearing and conversation, a gentleness and amiability in the art of pleasing, which was no growth of the English soil, but could only be acquired abroad. Most young Englishmen of condition were, in Lord Chesterfield's opinion, little more than louts: they had made indeed the grand tour abroad, but had learnt nothing from their travels, on which they had herded together in drunken debauches, returning home as refined and polished, he said, as Dutch skippers from a whaling expedition. That his son, and his godson and heir, to whom he addressed another series of instructive letters, should not resemble these unlicked cubs, but become accomplished young men, fitted to adorn their age and country, was Lord Chesterfield's great desire and the purpose of his letters. These letters were not, he said, the severe and discouraging dictates of an old parent, but the friendly and practicable advice of a sincere friend, who remembers that he has been young himself, and knows the indulgence that is due to youth and inexperience. "Yes," he adds, "I have been young, and a great deal too young. Idle dissipation and innumerable indiscretions, which I am now heartily ashamed and repent of, characterized my youth. But if my advice can make you wiser and better than I was at your age, I hope it may be some little atonement."

Lord Chesterfield's letters, which he wrote as an atonement for his youthful errors, and which to many have seemed a strange atonement, are full of worldly wisdom and advice which finds a terse expression in the many aphorisms which adorn their pages. Besides these scattered maxims, he composed for the instruction of his son a set of aphorisms which are printed by themselves.

"Most maxim-mongers," he says, in his preface to this collection, "have preferred the prettiness to the justness of a thought, and the turn to the truth; but I have refused myself to everything that my own experience did not justify and confirm." His aphorisms are indeed sincere expressions of his own thought and observation, but they are often little masterpieces of the literary art as well. Inheriting as he did his grandfather's gift for terse expression, and nourished as he was on La Rochefoucauld and La Bruyère, whom he continually quotes, and believing, as he believed, that form was as important as matter, and that indeed it was the form rather than the content of a phrase which impressed it upon us and fixed it in our memory, he had given a lifelong attention to the art of expressing thought in words. His aphorisms float sometimes on the wings of images—"Cunning," he says, for instance, "is the dark sanctuary of incapacity"; Wit, those who possess it, should wear like a sword in its scabbard, and not "brandish it to the terror of the whole company"; the art of life was to make the world one's bubble, rather than be the bubble of the world.

But of all the wings of winged sayings—and aphorisms must have wings to make them fly from mouth to mouth—the neatest are woven of a kind of verbal felicity, which Chesterfield called the "turn." The turn is generally a deft antithesis of phrasing, by which some antithesis of thought is echoed and reinforced. "It is very disagreeable to seem reserved, and very dangerous not to be so"; "The weakest man in the world can avail himself of the passions of the wisest"; "Many a man would rather you heard his story than granted his request"—these among many others are instances of the antithetical turn in Chesterfield's aphorisms. An antithesis is not, however, indispensable to the turn; often this verbal felicity is produced merely by the happy repetition of one word; —"Let blockheads read what blockheads wrote," for instance; "What pleases you in others will in general please them in you." In the art of using the turn Chesterfield's model was La Rochefoucauld, who sometimes combines the antithesis and the repetition in one finished phrase, as for instance when he says, "We can often forgive those who bore us, but we cannot forgive those we bore."

Although Lord Chesterfield was a master of the turn, he did not allow, as he says, the turn to be his master, and thus he avoided another pitfall of the aphorist, that of pretentiousness, of using a verbal felicity to give an appearance of thought where thought is lacking. When, for instance, Disraeli, who often fell into this pitfall, remarks "Nobody should ever look anxious except those who have no anxiety," the turn of expression he uses gives a momentary look of depth to an extremely shallow observation.

We have only to look at Sainte-Beuve's luminous portrait of Lord Chesterfield, with its sympathetic interpretation of this accomplished figure, to realize that our accepted notion of him is a caricature of the coarse old English kind. Sainte-Beuve, who calls Chesterfield the La Rochefoucauld of England, describes him as one of the most brilliant minds of our country, and as an accomplished moralist—using the word in the wider and more humane sense which it preserves in France—a moralist, not of Zeno's or Cato's school, but of the more amiable school of Aristippus or Atticus. His letters, Sainte-Beuve says, were letters that Horace might have written to his son, if Horace had been a parent; he praises the spirit they breathe of tenderness and wisdom, the paternal affection of this patient, delicate, indefatigable father, striving to make out of his indolent and awkward son an accomplished man of action. If, after reading the essay of this fine critic, we recall Dr. Johnson's saying that Lord Chesterfield's letters "teach the morals of a whore, and the manners of a dancing-master," we find ourselves in a very different critical and moral atmosphere. But even Dr. Johnson in a less exasperated mood was forced to admit that Chesterfield's correspondence, expurgated of what he considered its immoral precepts, would make a book which "should be put into the hands of every young gentleman."

Lord Chesterfield was supposed to have described Dr. Johnson as "a respectable Hottentot"; and the phrase, though apparently not meant for Johnson, was taken by their contemporaries as representing what the polite nobleman thought of the uncouth scholar. These two notable eighteenth-century figures lived indeed in worlds very different from each other; each was famous for his wit, but while Chesterfield regarded this quality as a possession dangerous for its possessor, Dr. Johnson, disporting himself in a less polished sphere, was hampered by no such scruples. To shine in conversation was in him, as Sir Joshua Reynolds said, a predominating passion; he fought on every occasion as if his reputation depended on the victory of the moment; and he fought with all the weapons. Among these he wielded with complete recklessness that shining sword of wit which the politic earl had said should be kept safely in its scabbard, and not brandished to the terror of the company. The strokes of this mighty Samson still reverberate in history; still he strides like great Hector sounding war's alarms among the dead; but we feel no pity for his victims. Time has changed into delight the terror of those lightning strokes of repartee; we listen safely across the intervening years to their thunder. But more than by his wit Dr. Johnson still lives for us, and his voice still reverberates in our ears, as the master and great monarch of wise sayings. He is the greatest of our English aphorists—indeed for the number, the originality of his apophthegms, he has no equal in the world; there is no talker of ancient or modern times of whose sayings so many are remembered and constantly repeated. We owe the profusion of this store, of course, to his indefatigable and incomparable biographer; but their most enduring quality is the immense common sense, and the weight of experience and feeling behind them. They have their sources in the depths of deeply-feeling nature; they are full of the knowledge of the good and evil in his own heart, and in the hearts of others. With this concrete experience of life was combined an extraordinary generalizing power, a wide grasp of thought, a power of applying general truths to particular occasions, of seeing little incidents in the illumination of large ideas, and of being inspired by them, as he said himself, to very serious reflections. A tub of butter when contemplated by the actor Munden amounted, Charles Lamb wrote, to a platonic idea; and the most trivial object or occurrence, when contemplated through the magnifying glass of Dr. Johnson's mind, assumed gigantic proportions; he went through life making mountains out of molehills. This gift of aggrandizement, of bestowing what he called the "grandeur of generality" upon his sayings, was due in part to a vocabulary which was the product as well as the organ of that gift. "He that thinks with more extent than another," he wrote, "will want words of larger meaning," and his store of sonorous Latinisms served well to express his extensive thoughts. This power of clothing his thoughts in words adequate to their ample meaning was the product of a lifelong effort; he had early made it a fixed rule, he told Sir Joshua Reynolds, "to do his best on every occasion and in every company; to impart whatever he knew in the most forcible language he could put it in"; and this had become, he said, by constant practice

habitual with him. "His notions," one of his lis-
teners writes, "rose up like the dragon's teeth sowed
by Cadmus, all ready clothed and in bright armour
too, fit for immediate battle"; and only occasionally
Boswell enables us to see him pausing for a moment
to give his thought a still more impressive form.

Dr. Johnson's aphoristic gift—and the power of
generalizing observation and abstracting from it imposing truths, is the very essence of that gift—is apparent
in his earlier writings, in *Rasselas* and the *Rambler;*
and his other essays are rich in the substance of aphoristic thought. Although the expression in these passages is often ponderous and diffuse, there are some of
them which, from their weight of meaning and the
neatness and perfection of their phrasing, deserve to
rank as aphorisms; for the aphorisms of La Rochefoucauld and the other masters of this art, though
generally brief and pointed, are sometimes more ample
in their form—paragraphs and almost little essays of
distilled and essential thought. No literary form
admits indeed of precise and strictly formal definition;
long sentences may be sometimes aphorisms; but the
briefer they are the better; and it is for the most part
in the recorded conversation of Dr. Johnson's later
years, when his weapon of speech had been tempered
in the fire and vociferation of innumerable verbal
contests, that his sentences acquire their final point
and perfection. Thus, for instance, in one of the
Ramblers he writes, "The time present is seldom able
to fill desire or imagination with immediate enjoyment, and we are forced to supply its deficiencies by
recollection or anticipation." Twenty-three years
later, arguing with Boswell and Langton at General
Oglethorpe's, he expressed this thought in a much

more vivid manner by saying "a man is never happy for the present, but when he is drunk."

There are no aphorisms that bear more clearly than Dr. Johnson's the impress of their maker; these massy coins are authentically stamped with his imposing wig and features. Johnson awed his contemporaries not only by the "loud voice and slow deliberate utterance" which Boswell so well describes; they were also impressed by the wit and wisdom of his remarks, but above all by the fact that it was he who made them. The weight of his extraordinary character, with all its amazing contradictions, gives them a resonance and importance that strongly affects us. Most sages and most aphorists have achieved a consistent attitude towards life; like La Rochefoucauld or like Chesterfield, or like Goethe, they have mastered both themselves and the world, small or large, in which they dwell, and this gives a kind of uniformity—sometimes a kind of monotony—to their sayings. But Dr. Johnson had achieved no such harmony; he was not in this sense a master of the world or of his own nature. He lived, as he tells us, entirely without his own approbation; he was continually forming resolutions and continually breaking them; and it is Boswell's supreme merit that he had the courage to reveal the contradictions and failings of his hero's character. High acts and noble qualities may win our respectful admiration, but it is after all people's errors, as Goethe said, which make us love them; and some of Johnson's eulogists have wronged his memory by trying to make him into a consistently enlightened figure. Johnson was fond also of paradox, and his most paradoxical remarks were accurately recorded; and when Boswell, wishing to be sure that none of them should escape him, inquired whether he had said that "the happiest part of a man's life is what he passes lying awake in bed in the morning," Dr. Johnson replied, "I may perhaps have said this; for nobody, at times, talks more laxly than I do."

The self-confessed contradictions between Dr. Johnson's principles and his practice—the way, for instance, he preached, and, as he said, very sincerely preached, early-rising from an habitual bed of noon-day sloth —and all the other contrarieties of his character; his liberal sympathies and his fierce, narrow, party-spirit, his profound unhappiness and his amazing zest for life, his bluff common sense and his primitive superstition, and almost insane terror of death—all these contrasts, and the various vistas into life they opened for him, enabled him to grasp those glimmerings of truth and odd aspects of experience which are the aphorist's nutriment—the game he hunts, and the object of his pursuit. But of all the contradictions of Dr. Johnson's nature, what makes him our supremest aphorist as well as most endears us to him, is the contrast between his craving for affection, his dependence on it, and his profound sense of the weakness and fragility of all human ties. "We cannot be in his company long," as Mr. Desmond MacCarthy has finely said, "without becoming aware that what draws us to him so closely is that he combined a disillusioned estimate of human nature sufficient to launch twenty little cynics, with a craving for love and sympathy urgent enough to turn a weaker nature into a benign sentimentalist."

The next aphorist on our list, though a younger contemporary of Chesterfield and Johnson, seems to belong to an age very different from theirs.

If a saying can create a world—and the universe we inhabit was thus, we are told, originally created—one saying of William Blake's seems to transport us into a sphere of thought and feeling as remote from that of these eighteenth-century figures as the farthest planet. Blake's aphorisms in *The Marriage of Heaven and Hell*, with the other aphorisms scattered through his prose writings, are indeed remarkable achievements, and contain, as Swinburne said of them, the quintessence and fine gold of his alembic. "Each, whether earnest or satirical, slight or great in manner, is full," Swinburne adds, "of that passionate wisdom and bright rapid strength proper to the step and speech of gods." Swinburne seldom indulged in understatement; but Blake's "Proverbs of Hell" are certainly little masterpieces of this delicate art. No other aphorist has succeeded in compressing greater depths of meaning into fewer words; and save for a few apophthegms of the Greek Sages—"Know thyself," "Seize the moment," "It is hard to be good," "Most men are bad"—it would be difficult to find in any literature sayings more brief and pointed than "Damn braces. Bless relaxes," and many other of Blake's tiny but pregnant maxims.

The ground covered by Blake's aphorisms includes the three kinds of experience which, as we have seen, form the subject matter of this way of writing. Some of them are commonplaces, new-minted and given a fresh lustre by their phrasing and imagery: "The busy bee has no time for sorrow"; "The fox condemns the trap, not himself," for instance. Others contain bits of experience with which we are not unacquainted, though no one else has embodied them in words. But Blake's most characteristic sayings belong to that rarest

D

and most precious class which seem like new intuitions—seem to have been coined from a vein of gold hidden far below the surface of the familiar world: "The soul of sweet delight can never be defiled," for instance; "Weak is the joy which is never wearied"—"The road of excess leads to the palace of wisdom." Blake is remarkable among aphorists in many ways, but most remarkable in that his proverbs have often a mysterious oracular quality; they seem to us pregnant with a kind of mystic meaning, although we are hard put to it to say exactly what that meaning is. "One thought fills immensity"; "The tigers of wrath are wiser than the horses of instruction"; "Eternity is in love with the productions of time"—phrases like these impress our imagination with a kind of awe, although reason may suggest that they are perhaps little more than nonsense phrases. But Blake is a poet among our great aphorists; his phrases were coined in the mint of the imagination, he speaks not with the voice of disillusioned age, but with that of romantic youth; and it is in reading one of his sentences, full of light and poetry, that we can best appreciate La Bruyère's saying that "a delicate thought is the finest product, and, as it were, the flower of the soul."

After Blake we return with Hazlitt to the flat earth again, and to the realm of reason; we listen again to that chorus of voices which, since before the time of Ecclesiastes, has been crying "Vanity, all is vanity" in our ears. Hazlitt was in many ways as disillusioned as Dr. Johnson, but he was, as Johnson was not, bitter and sardonic, and he hated rather than loved his fellow human beings. But his zest for life was even greater than that of Johnson, or was nourished at least by a wider variety of pleasures; the joys of solitude, of walking, of travel, of violent games, of outdoor life and physical exertion added for him an intoxicating taste to the bitter draught of experience. And Hazlitt, though no poet, breathed the enchanted atmosphere of the great age of poetry in which he lived, while Rousseau, of whom he was a fervent disciple, had opened his eyes to the strange and deeply coloured beauty of the world which shone about him. He was a painter, too, and no one could derive a greater joy from a picture or a lovely landscape. "The contemplation of truth and beauty is the proper object for which we were created, which calls forth the most intense desires of the soul, and of which it never tires"—a sentence like this, which would have sounded like cant in the eighteenth-century ears of Dr. Johnson, was nevertheless the expression of what was no mere aspiration, but the essential reality of a life otherwise so sordid, so acrid and unhappy.

Another romantic element in Hazlitt's nature, which would also have seemed like cant to Dr. Johnson, was his passionate love of liberty; his hope, in spite of his knowledge of "that toad-eating animal, man," for a reign of kindness and reason which might be ultimately established on the earth. His cry "O Reason! when will thy long minority expire?" is a genuine expression of this hope which he still cherished, although he well knew that, as he put it, "if mankind had wished for what is right, they might have had it long ago." Hazlitt, unlike Johnson, was a deliberate writer of aphorisms,[1]

---

[1] Dr. Johnson had however planned, among other schemes he never carried out, making a collection of "Maxims, Characters, and Sentiments, after the manner of Bruyère, collected out of ancient authours, particularly the Greek, with Apophthegms." (*Life*, iv, p. 382).

and a careful student of this form of literary art. In 1823 he published anonymously a volume of them entitled *Characteristics; in the Manner of Rochefoucault's Maxims*. He had been so struck, he tells us in the perusal of these French maxims, by the force and beauty of the style and matter, that he felt an earnest desire to embody some occasional thoughts of his own in the same form; and having written a few, both the novelty and the agreeableness of the task impelled him forward. In addition to the *Characteristics*, Hazlitt also printed in various magazines three other collections. Along with all these separate collections, Hazlitt, like other authors with the aphoristic gift, enriched all his writings, his essays, and his *Life of Napoleon* with such an abundance of terse sayings that, were they all put together, they would probably exceed in number those of any other English writer, with the exception of Dr. Johnson. Their quality is on the whole a high one; although they seldom possess that occasional surprise of diction which delights us in so many of Johnson's sayings, and are lacking also in the stamp of his warm and human character, they are often terse and profound and pointed, and, unlike Johnson, he often makes use of the "turn" to give them wings. "It is the business of reviewers to watch poets, not of poets to watch reviewers"; "There is a pleasure in madness, which none but madmen know"—phrases like these recall the aphorisms of his French masters, or those of Chesterfield, their other English pupil. Hazlitt also reminds us of French writers like Chamfort in the occasional bitterness, the almost vitriolic quality of some of his aphorisms. Old friendships, he says, are like stale food, "the stomach turns against them"; "We grow tired," he says

36

again, "of everything but turning others into ridicule, and congratulating ourselves on their defects."

After Hazlitt, Emerson is the next, and with one exception, the last great aphorist who has written in English. Emerson's note-books are full of detached thoughts and intuitions—the berries and wild fruit, as he called them, which he found in his basket after endless rambles in the New England woods and meadows. When he came to write an essay or address, he would turn to these note-books for ideas and phrases more or less relevant to the subject he had chosen. His essays are, therefore, like Bacon's, a mosaic of detached thoughts and aphorisms; they are not organized compositions, but glimpses of truth, as he described them; flashes of light followed by obscurity, and then another flash; each sentence, as he said himself, an infinitely repellent particle. The interest and value of his writings is to be found therefore in these clearly-cut medallions of thought, these brief and pregnant phrases.

With the exception of Halifax, Emerson is the only writer in our language who has given his best care and attention to the detached—and the detachable—sentence; he is a master of the polished and perfected phrase. For all his decorum, benevolence and apparent mildness, Emerson, like other aphorists, was also, like Halifax, caustic and keen-sighted, and often drew upon that accumulated store of disillusion which this way of writing seems best fitted to express. "A person seldom falls sick, but the bystanders are animated with a faint hope that he will die"; "We do not quite forgive a giver. The hand that feeds us is in some danger of being bitten"—sentences like these read like some of the most cynical of La Rochefoucauld's maxims.

But to write of Emerson as a cynic and pessimist would be to absurdly misrepresent him. He could dip his pen in the blackest ink, because he was not, he said, afraid of falling into the inkpot. His spirit was loving and benevolent; his disillusion and ironic observation was softened, and sometimes too much softened, by his idealism and ignorance of evil; and although he found that there was a crack in everything God had made, and some foible in every man, however saintly, he put his conclusions in terms with so much humaneness in their daring, that they seem to add more to the gaiety than to the sadness of the human spectacle. In the sentence, "Let us treat the men and women well: treat them as if they were real: perhaps they are," he expressed both his disillusion and his tolerance for human beings—"chafed and irritable creatures with red faces" that we are.

As an aphorist Emerson ranks more with Blake than with any of our other writers of thoughts and maxims; in his sayings, as in Blake's, we find at its richest the imaginative quality of the English aphorism. "We think our civilization near its meridian, but we are yet only at the cock-crowing and the morning star" —this and other characteristic phrases are luminous with a kind of poetic radiance, less brilliant than the flashing sunlight of Blake's genius, but more serene, more like the illumination of the stars, "the delicately emerging stars," to borrow one of his own phrases, "with their private and ineffable glances."

But Emerson was a preacher, the son and descendant of a line of preachers, and if his sentences escape, and some of them cannot be said to escape—being hortatory truisms, this is due partly to their imaginative phrasing, but still more to a certain humour which stamps them as his own, and a kind of provincial quaintness in their expression. It is unfortunate that the habit of oral delivery, of lecturing to uncultivated audiences about the country, led him to exaggerate this quaintness of expression, and somewhat strain and crack his voice. His best sentences are often to be found therefore in those journals in which he jotted down his thoughts and intuitions—the deposit, drop by drop, and day by day, of the lifelong soliloquy of his mind. In his lectures and in his essays (which were delivered as lectures) a forced poetic note can sometimes be detected, a kind of shrill rhetoric, which obscures for too many readers that profundity of thought, and that occasional perfection of phrasing which makes him rank as by no means the least important in that succession of great aphorists who have contributed to our literature so rich, so varied, and so disregarded a store of wise, pungent or poetic sayings.

In addition to these writers—Bacon, Selden, Halifax, Johnson, Blake, Hazlitt, and Emerson, there are several minor English aphorists who may be more briefly noticed. First in date among these is Ben Jonson, whose prose *Discoveries* are rich in pointed and profound sayings, and then James Harrington, the author of *Oceana*, who embodied, in two sets of aphorisms, his wise and liberal reflections on the troubled politics of his time. Three divines of the Church of England must also be mentioned: Thomas Fuller, Jeremy Taylor, and Thomas Wilson, Bishop of Sodor and Man. That miscellaneous and amusing writer Thomas Fuller published among his numerous writings three series of "Thoughts"—*Good Thoughts in Bad Times* (1645), *Good Thoughts in Worse Times* (1647), both written during the Civil Wars, and *Mixt*

Contemplations on Better Times, published at the Restoration. The "Thoughts" which make up these volumes are, like the numerous "Maxims" of his *Holy and Profane State*, little essays and reflections, and belong to that way of writing in detached paragraphs which the French call *Pensées*, but for which, though abundant in our literature, we have no generally accepted name. But among these Reflections or Laconics—and the old word "Laconics" is perhaps our best appellation for this way of writing—we find, as in all of Fuller's other writings, many aphoristic sentences, brief, pointed and often winged with the quaint images which floated in such multitudes amid his wandering thoughts. "Miracles are the swaddling-clothes of infant churches"; "A fool's Paradise is a wise man's hell"; "Anger is one of the sinews of the soul"; "Pastime, like wine, is poison in the morning," are examples of these brief and vivid phrases, and of the quaint originality of his way of thinking which gives an amusing twist to many of his sayings.

Our second divine is that great prose-poet Jeremy Taylor, who, though his meaning was for the most part too richly adorned with splendid images to be bottled in a tiny phrase, yet gives us now and then in a brief and shining sentence the essence of his thought. "Virtue," he says, for instance, "is like hunger or thirst; it must be satisfied or we die." "He that loves not his wife and children, feeds a Lioness at home, and broods a nest of sorrow," is a sentence on married life in one of his sermons, and writing on the same subject in his *Holy Living* he picturesquely tells us, "Better sit up all night, than go to bed with a Dragon."

Thomas Wilson, Bishop of Sodor and Man, who was born in 1663, and died in 1755, was, like Lord

Halifax, a deliberate writer of aphorisms; and in his
Sacra Privata and his *Maxims of Piety and of Christianity*
we possess two large collections of pious and edifying
maxims. Wilson is principally remembered—as far
as he is at all remembered—by the praise given by
Matthew Arnold to this holy bishop, who united,
Matthew Arnold says, the most sincere ardour and
unction "to that downright honesty and plain good
sense which our English race has so powerfully applied
to the divine impossibilities of religion." Wilson's
maxims, his "valuable precepts and admonitions of
piety," as Matthew Arnold calls them, have often a
perfection of form which distinguishes them from the
general run of pious reflections. But this art, with its
taint of original sin—and it was by means of an aphoristic phrase that Satan tempted Eve—seems to have got
the better of Bishop Wilson, as it did of Bishop Taylor,
now and then. "Love is a talkative passion" is a
saying which his episcopal pen might innocently let
drop, but on opening his *Maxims of Piety and Christianity*, we are surprised to find him saying, "When we
attend a funeral, we are apt to comfort ourselves with
the happy difference there is betwixt us and our dead
friend." Even less edifying, and we must hope less
true, is the remark on the first page of this volume:
"How many are raised to high posts in the Church by
the instigation of the devil, that their fall may be more
dismal!"

In addition to these divines, there are three other
seventeenth-century writers, Hobbes, Milton, and Sir
Thomas Browne, whose writings I have drawn upon
in compiling this book The works of Hobbes are
rich in aphoristic thought, but he seldom expressed
it with aphoristic terseness; while Milton's prose

reflections are almost all too ample, and too amply embroidered, for us to call him an "aphorismer," in a word of his own coining. Browne is more deserving of the appellation, for although his meditations hover, for the most part, on vast and dusky wings, they are sometimes brief and pointed in their expression. Another seventeenth-century writer, Samuel Butler, the author of *Hudibras*, was a more deliberate writer of aphorisms, and his works contain a collection of them which are not, however, of much interest or importance.

William Penn's *Some Fruits of Solitude, in Reflections and Maxims*, which was published anonymously in 1693, with the *More Fruits of Solitude* published in 1718, are collections of aphoristic sayings which enjoyed immense popularity in their time, and which Robert Louis Stevenson rediscovered and cherished with a peculiar enthusiasm. The ground for this enthusiasm is somewhat difficult to understand, as the reflections of the good Quaker show no great profundity of observation or subtlety of thought. Penn seems, however, to have studied La Rochefoucauld's maxims, and to have learned from him a certain neatness of expression, as when he says, for instance, "They have a Right to censure, that have a Heart to help"; "Equivocation is half-way to Lying, as Lying the whole way to Hell"; "Every Stroke our Fury strikes is sure to hit ourselves at last."

Of somewhat more interest is another contemporary aphorist who was also popular in his time, although he is completely forgotten now. This is a certain Dr. Thomas Fuller, whose writings have been sometimes confused with those of Thomas Fuller, the celebrated divine, with whom, however, he seems not to have been connected save by name, and possibly by some remote tie of kinship. Dr. Fuller, who was born in 1654 and died at the age of eighty in 1734, spent his life as a physician at Sevenoaks in Kent, and toward the end of his long career wrote a collection of 3,152 maxims, counsels and cautions, for the instruction of his son John, and the guidance through life of this well-advised young man. Many of these maxims are borrowed from other moralists, from the great store of didactic platitudes which has been accumulating ever since the dawn of moral reflection; there are others, however, which bear a more individual stamp, and seem to be the mellowed fruit of Dr. Fuller's own experience —the experience of a wise, old, convivial, comfort-loving doctor in a country town. On almost every subject—on Friendship, Love, Marriage, Money, and Ambition, his maxims embody a singularly complete and practicable kind of wisdom. Young Fuller was admonished to think above all of his own comfort, to avoid ambition and the desire to play a leading part among his neighbours; he should marry a wife with money, and not too much money; he should shun the acquaintance of persons of high rank, whom it was easy, but extremely dangerous, to offend. Still greater care must he take to avoid making friends with poor people—the old doctor is most emphatic on this point; he himself had had several friends of this kind, whose endless sorrows and necessities had made him uneasy, and spoilt for him the enjoyment of his own money. Dr. Fuller's maxims, though they embody an ideal of life which is not at all heroic, are full nevertheless of a shrewd and cautious kind of worldly wisdom which is often expressed in happy images and phrases. His books of maxims do not quite deserve the oblivion which has overtaken them. There is a dim light on their didactic pages of a kind of golden mediocrity, a mediocrity of ease and quiet and good food in a comfortable old house in Sevenoaks in Kent; and it is pleasant to think of the octogenarian doctor prosing away on summer afternoons to his deferential son, two hundred years ago.

The writing of aphorisms became something of a fashion in the eighteenth century. Lord Shaftesbury shows in many a sentence of his *Characteristics* that he, like the French duke, and like Lords Halifax and Chesterfield, was a master of this aristocratic art; and Swift and Pope and Shenstone all left behind them collections of aphoristic sayings. Those of Swift are admirable in their sardonic terseness; Pope's are fewer; he possessed the aphoristic turn of mind, but employed it chiefly in his verses. When, however, he says, "A family is but too often a commonwealth of malignants," he shows that he could have expressed himself, had he wished to do so, in vitriolic prose. The aphorisms of another poet, Shenstone, are much more numerous, and are not lacking in observation of others and himself. But though his coins possess a certain weight, lustre is for the most part lacking; there is little distinction in their form and phrasing.

Aphoristic writing fell out of fashion in the nineteenth century; with the exception of Hazlitt and Emerson, none of its authors have paid much attention to this art. Hazlitt indeed describes Coleridge as spending his life in the momentary pursuit of truths as they were butterflies; and this pursuit, he adds, was Coleridge's chief faculty as well as pleasure. We possess several collections of Coleridge's thoughts and sayings, but these are, in their form, more brief essays or laconics than aphorisms, and with few exceptions we do not find among them many terse and pointed phrases. This is true also of the prose of his contemporaries, Keats and Shelley, in which, however, we catch now and then the gleam of some gnomic and yet golden phrase.

From the writings of Disraeli and Oscar Wilde collections of sayings and maxims have been made; but Disraeli's pretentious aphorisms, and Oscar Wilde's paradoxes (for all their shining wit) must for the most part be classed among the counterfeit currency of thought. George Eliot's novels are rich in aphoristic wisdom; her mind had a width and depth something like that of Goethe's, but she lacked for the most part Goethe's power of terse expression, although in Mrs. Poyser she created the only female aphorist of whom our literature can boast. Another novelist, George Meredith, was a lover of aphorisms, and those he too sparely quotes from the *Egoist's Handbook*, and from the *Pilgrim's Scrip* of Sir Austin Feverel, make us wish that we possessed more treasures from these imaginary collections. Of all our story-tellers, Robert Louis Stevenson was the most accomplished aphorist; he was a writer of moral essays as well as of fiction, and in these essays can be found many witty and wise sayings.

Three other nineteenth-century writers must be mentioned who were endowed with the aphoristic turn of thought; the first of these is Sir Henry Taylor, a poet whose play, *Philip van Artevelde*, is still remembered. Taylor was also an eminent Civil Servant and successful man of affairs, and for some strange reason it occurred to him to tell the truth about worldly success and how it is obtained—to describe the methods, the arts and even the tricks by means of which ambitious men achieve, or try to achieve, the objects of their ambition. In this book, which he called *The Statesman*, and which was a cause, among statesmen, of considerable scandal, he condensed in brief aphoristic phrases much of that worldly wisdom which has so often found expression in an aphoristic literature. Sir Henry Taylor, when he found how much right-thinking people had been scandalized by his *Statesman*, pretended that he had written it with an ironic intention; but his maxims, like those of Chesterfield, possess a kind of weight and cynical integrity, as if he had embodied in them the frank expression of genuine experience, and had not, like most aphorists, made any attempt to be amusing or plausible or clever or ironic.

Of equal interest are the wise and pregnant sentences which abound in the writings of Walter Bagehot, that country banker who was not only the profoundest political thinker of his time, but also an accomplished painter of moral portraits and a penetrating critic of literature as well. Samuel Butler, the author of *Erewhon*, like Samuel Butler, the author of *Hudibras*, was a copious writer of thoughts and reflections, but his *Note-Books*, like those of Coleridge, are more reflections and tiny essays than aphorisms, although they contain a certain number of famous and terse phrases. Coventry Patmore's *The Rod, the Root and the Flower* is a collection of detached religious meditations, which are hardly aphorisms; his biographer, however, has printed a number of briefer sayings of point and interest.

In other Victorian biographies, Rossetti's *Life*, and Benjamin Jowett's *Letters*, we find other collections of sayings; Rossetti's are not very characteristic; the connoisseur in these matters would hardly attribute without evidence to the author of the *Blessed Damozel* the remark, "No skunk can get rid of his own name by giving it to another." The sayings of the famous Master of Balliol bear a more authentic stamp of his own image: "Young men make great mistakes in life; for one thing they idealize love too much"; "I hope our young men will not grow into such *dodgers* as these old men are. I believe everything that a *young* man says to me"; "Nowhere probably is there more true feeling, and nowhere worse taste, than in a churchyard";— Jowett's surviving friends and pupils will recognize in these sayings the acute accents of the Master's voice.

Of all these collected sayings in Victorian biographies those that Mrs. Creighton has printed in her life of Bishop Creighton are of the greatest interest and value. The late Bishop of London was, as Dean Inge has pointed out, a gifted aphorist; and when Creighton remarks, "No people do so much harm as those who go about doing good," adding, however, for our consolation, "It is wonderful how little mischief we can do with all our trouble," we learn, as we learned from Bishop Wilson, that English prelates when they take to writing aphorisms can be quite as caustic as the lay masters of this form.

Dean Inge has also called attention to the aphorisms of Churton Collins, "an able critic," Dean Inge remarks, "who, I believe, did not show much worldly wisdom in his conduct of affairs." Some of Churton Collins' aphorisms—"Never trust a man who speaks well of everybody," for instance, "A wise man, like the moon, only shows his bright side to the world," make us regret that of the hundreds of aphorisms which, his biographer tells us, Churton Collins wrote, only a small number have been given to the world.

The late F. H. Bradley has printed a few—too few—philosophical aphorisms in the preface of his *Appearance and Reality*; but another and living philosopher, Mr. Santayana, remains to show that this delicate art, so difficult and so full of perils, is not yet among the perished arts, since one of its masters is still living. Mr. Mackail's writings show that he also possesses this gift, although he rarely exercises it.   Mr. Bernard Shaw's witty *Maxims for Revolutionists* in *Man and Superman* are well known; he is, I believe, among living writers the only one who has published a collection of detached aphoristic sentences.

I have arranged the aphorisms of our famous aphorists—and those too of other English writers who like Dryden and Gibbon cannot be counted as aphorists, although they occasionally expressed their thought in terse phrases—I have arranged all these aphorisms and maxims and sayings under certain general heads.   The book begins with a section on the aphorism itself, what our aphorists have said about this way of writing, its material, its forms, its advantages, its perils and its drawbacks.   Then follow their sayings about the universe and the life and status on this planet of "that good, that bad"—as one of our aphorists described him—"that knowing, that ignorant, that reasoning and unreasonable creature, Man."   This incomprehensible being has been always the main object for the observation, moral or satiric, of gnomic writers; and his activities, as Dr. Johnson said, will furnish "the materials of speculation to the end of time."

In the first section of this book, man is considered more as an isolated being than as a member of society, and the faculties, passions, virtues and vices, the griefs, and pleasures and experiences of the individual in youth and age, in happiness or sorrow, form in the main their subject matter. But Man is above all a social and political animal; his relations with his fellow human beings form his most absorbing and important interest. His more intimate ties of friendship, of love, marriage and the family claim us first, and then his relations, in all their infinite complexity, with the many-peopled world in which he plays his successful or ineffectual part. The passions of envy, anger and emulation aroused by his encounter with the world, the fools and knaves he meets there, the arts by which he circumvents them, and the worldly prudence that should guide him, form the subject matter of those worldly counsels in which our English aphorists abound. They seem to regard verbal encounters as of especial interest and importance, and to almost more than any other subject they have given their attention to the clash of tongues. "A man is made by conversation," Dr. Johnson said; his talk may establish or undo him in the world. A sage courtier of the Chinese empire once boasted that with his "five inches of tongue" he had won his way to greatness in the great world; and this world of kings and courts, of ceremony and pageants, of wealth and vanity and fashion, has been the subject of much moral as well as worldly observation; while to the aphorists of so political a race as the English, the subject of power and politics has always aroused, of course, a special interest.

Contrasted with these worlds are those of learning and literature and art and religion; and finally the great subject of death engages our attention, with which this sententious creature vanishes from the scene of his

E

activities, leaving behind him a few memorable comments upon himself, and his experience. How interesting a collection of these comments we possess in our language will, I hope, be apparent from the following pages; and if the French are famous for the lucid perfection of their winged sayings, we may take pride in the far greater variety of our native species—in all the many-coloured butterflies and dusky moths of English imaginative thought.

I

THE APHORISM

THERE is a certain list of vices committed in all ages, and declaimed against by all Authors, which will last as long as human nature; or digested into commonplaces may serve for any theme, and never be out of date until Doomsday.

Sir Thomas Browne, V, 22.

A MAN that should call every thing by its right Name, would hardly pass the Streets without being knocked down as a common Enemy. *Halifax*, 246.

I FANCY mankind may come, in time, to write all aphoristically, except in narrative; grow weary of preparation, and connection, and illustration, and all those arts by which a big book is made.

Dr. Johnson, B, V, 39.

WHO hath sailed about the world of his own heart, sounded each creek, surveyed each corner, but that still there remains therein much *terra incognita* to himself? *Thomas Fuller, H*, 34.

LIFE is not the object of science; we see a little, very little. *Dr. Johnson, A*, No. 107.

To most men, experience is like the stern lights of a ship, which illumine only the track it has passed.

Coleridge, T T, 434.

MOST maxim-mongers have preferred the prettiness to the justness of a thought, and the turn to the truth; but I have refused myself to everything that my own experience did not justify and confirm.

Chesterfield, 569.

THE preposterous notions of a systematical man, who does not know the world, tire the patience of a man who does. *Chesterfield*, 579.

WOULD you know the characters, modes, and manners of the latter end of the last age, which are very like those of the present, read La Bruyère. But would you know man, independently of modes, read La Rochefoucault, who, I am afraid, paints him very exactly. *Ibid.*, 403.

ALL which, Sir, though I most powerfully and potently believe, yet I hold it not honesty to have it thus set down.

Hamlet, II, ii.

THAT observation which is called knowledge of the world will be found much more frequently to make men cunning than good.

Dr. Johnson, R, No. 4.

THE mind of man, when its daily maxims are put before it, revolts from anything so stupid, so mean, so poor. *Bagehot, L*, II, 266.

MUCH of the wisdom of the world is not wisdom.

Emerson, E, I, 155.

A THOUGHT must tell at once, or not at all.

Hazlitt, C, VI.

To repeat what has been said a thousand times is commonplace; to contradict it because it has been so said, is not originality.

Ibid., W, I, 381.

PARADOXES are useful to attract attention to ideas.
Bishop Creighton, L.

IN all pointed sentences, some degree of accuracy must be sacrificed to conciseness.
Dr. Johnson, W, X, 286.

ALMOST every wise saying has an opposite one, no less wise, to balance it. *Santayana, E,* 237.

IN every work of genius we recognize our own rejected thoughts; they come back to us with a certain alienated majesty. *Emerson, E,* I, 23.

I DIP my pen in the blackest ink, because I am not afraid of falling into my inkpot.
Ibid., II, 296.

WHEN what should be greatest truths flat out into shallow truisms, then we are all sick.
Ibid., J, IV, 30.

NEVER utter the truism, but live it among men.
Ibid., J, III, 455.

TRUTH is a jewel which should not be painted over; but it may be set to advantage and shown in a good light. *Santayana, R,* IV, 105.

BEWARE of cultivating this delicate art.
Lord Morley, Studies in Literature, 88.

IF thou intendest to live happy, thou must make but few Reflections on Life.
Dr. Fuller, II, 157.

LET not England forget her precedence of teaching Nations how to live. *Milton,* I, 278.

II

THE UNIVERSE

THAT which once existed in intellect as pure law, has now taken body as Nature. It existed already in the mind in solution; now, it has been precipitated, and the bright sediment is the world.

Emerson, E, III, 433.

SOMETHING inherently mean in action! Even the creation of the universe disturbs my idea of the Almighty's greatness. *Coleridge, A, 27.*

THE world, which took but six days to make, is like to take six thousand to make out.

Sir Thomas Browne, C, 62.

THE world was made to be inhabited by Beasts, but studied and contemplated by man.

Ibid., R, 25.

'TIS wondrous to contemplate the world emptied of all intelligence. *Bishop Berkeley, 59.*

LET us interrogate the great apparition, that shines so peacefully around us.

Emerson, E, II, 371.

WE are startled to find a universe we did not expect.

Bagehot, L, II, 403.

THE universe, as far as we can observe it, is a wonderful and immense engine; its extent, its order, its beauty, its cruelty, make it alike impressive. If we dramatize its life and conceive its spirit, we are filled with wonder, terror, and amusement, so magnificent is that spirit, so prolific, inexorable, grammatical and dull.

Santayana, E, 85.

GREAT is this organism of mud and fire, terrible this vast, painful, glorious experiment.

Santayana, E, 86.

"NATURE in late centuries," says Sauerteig, "was universally supposed to be dead; an old eight-day clock, made many thousand years ago, and still ticking, but dead as brass,—which the Maker, at most, sat looking at, in a distant, singular and indeed incredible manner."

Carlyle, Past and Present, I, v.

THE existing world is not a dream, and cannot with impunity be treated as a dream.

Emerson, E, III, 491.

REALITY, however, has a sliding floor.

Ibid., J, X, 365.

CHILDREN, it is true, believe in the external world. The belief that it appears only, is an afterthought.

Ibid., E, II, 405.

THOUGH the world exist from thought, thought is daunted in presence of the world

Ibid., 364.

THERE is a crack in everything God has made.

Ibid., I, 57.

TAKEN as a whole, the universe is absurd. There seems an unalterable contradiction between the human mind and its employments.

Bagehot, L, I, 36.

WE all live together in a world that is bursting with sin and sorrow.

Dr. Johnson, M, I, 301.

WHERE everything is bad it must be good to know the worst.

F. H. Bradley, XV.

WHERE all is rotten it is a man's work to cry stinking fish.

Ibid.

ONE real world is enough.

Santayana, E, 31.

WE are told that when Jehovah created the world he saw that it was good. What would he say now?

Bernard Shaw, 241.

ETERNITY is in love with the productions of time.

Blake.

AND time and space,—what are they? Our first problems, which we ponder all our lives through, and leave where we found them; whose outrunning immensity, the old Greeks believed, astonished the gods themselves; of whose dizzy vastitudes all the worlds of God are a mere dot on the margin; impossible to deny, impossible to believe.

Emerson, E, III, 299.

IF the stars should appear one night in a thousand years, how would men believe and adore!

Ibid., II, 373.

THE good globe is faithful, and carries us securely through the celestial spaces, anxious or resigned; we need not interfere to help it on.

Ibid., E, I, 353.

THE solar system has no anxiety about its reputation.

Ibid., II, 297.

IF you go expressly to look at the moon, it becomes tinsel.

Emerson, J, IV, 80.

FOR the world, I count it not an Inn, but an Hospital, and a place, not to live, but to die in.

Sir Thomas Browne, R, 162.

IF the world were good for nothing else, it is a fine subject for speculation.

Hazlitt, C, 108.

III

LIFE

PHILOSOPHER! Let me hear concerning what is of some moment to me. Let me hear concerning *Life*; what the right Notion is; and what I am to stand to, upon occasion; that I may not, when Life seems retiring, or has run itself out to the very Dregs, cry "Vanity!"; condemn the World, and at the same time complain "that Life is short and passing." For why so short, indeed, if not found sweet? Why do I complain both ways? Is Vanity, mere Vanity, a Happiness? Or can Misery pass away too soon?

Shaftesbury, I, 302.

LIFE is a pill which none of us can bear to swallow without gilding.

Dr. Johnson, M, I, 205.

WE are always getting ready to live, but never living.
Emerson, J, III, 276.

LIFE is not a spectacle or a feast; it is a predicament.
Santayana, V.

WE seldom see anybody who is not uneasy or afraid to live. Emerson, E, I, 512.

LIFE is like playing a violin solo in public and learning the instrument as one goes on.

Samuel Butler, E, 93.

WHEN all is done, human life is, at the greatest and the best, but like a froward child, that must be played with and humoured a little to keep it quiet, till it falls asleep, and then the care is over.

Sir William Temple, of Poetry.

WE have but a bad bargain, God knows, of this life, and patience is the only way not to make bad worse.
Chesterfield, 1330.

LIFE is barren enough surely with all her trappings; let us therefore be cautious how we strip her.
Dr. Johnson, M, I, 345.

HE that lives longest lives but a little while.
Ibid., R, No. 71.

SURELY life, if it be not long, is tedious, since we are forced to call in the assistance of so many trifles to rid us of our time.
Ibid., B, I, 363.

A YEAR is no contemptible portion of this mortal existence.
Gibbon, M, I, p. 644.

A DAY is a miniature Eternity.
Emerson, J, IV, 26.

THOSE who complain of the shortness of life, let it slide by them without wishing to seize and make the most of its golden minutes.
Hazlitt, S A, 336.

HE that calculates the growth of trees, has the unwelcome remembrance of the shortness of life driven hard upon him.
Dr. Johnson, W, X, 490.

IN seventy or eighty years, a man may have a deep gust of the world; know what it is, what it can afford, and what 'tis to have been a man.
Sir Thomas Browne, C, 119.

59

THE business of Life is to go forwards.
Dr. Johnson, Idler, No. 72.

LIFE is a school of probability.
Bagehot, L, II, 257.

WHY should not things be largely absurd, futile and transitory? They are so, and we are so, and they and we go very well together.
Santayana, V.

SANITY is a madness put to good uses; waking life is a dream controlled.
Ibid., E, 146.

LIFE consists in what a man is thinking of all day.
Emerson, J, VII, 319.

A MAN cannot spend all this life in frolick.
Dr. Johnson, R, No. 31.

LIFE is one long process of getting tired.
Samuel Butler, N, 11.

ALMOST every person, if you will believe himself, holds a quite different theory of life from the one on which he is patently acting.
R. L. Stevenson, V, 203.

OUR modes of living are not agreeable to our imagination.
Emerson, E, III, 475.

WHAT a deal of cold business doth a man mis-spend the better part of life in! In scattering compliments, tendering visits, gathering and venting news, following feasts and plays, making a little winter-love in a dark corner.
Ben Jonson, 390.

OH that men would seek immortal moments!
Blake, L, I, 65.

LIFE is a pure flame, and we live by an invisible Sun
within us.   *Sir Thomas Browne, U,* 29.

THE contemplation of truth and beauty is the proper
object for which we were created, which calls forth
the most intense desires of the soul, and of which it
never tires.   *Hazlitt, A,* I, 2.

THE mind soars to the lofty: it is at home in the grovel-
ling, the disagreeable, and the little.
Ibid., W S, 77.

To what a point of insignificance may not human life
dwindle! To what fine, agonizing threads will it
not cling!
Ibid., L R, II, 246.

ONCE I supposed that only my manner of living was
superficial; that all other men's was solid.   Now I find
we are all alike shallow.
Emerson, J, V, 198.

WE live ruins amidst ruins.
Ibid., E, III, 58.

To live is like to love—all reason is against it, and all
healthy instinct for it.
Samuel Butler, N, 227.

THE race of mankind have always offered at least this
implied thanks for the gift of existence,—namely, the
terror of its being taken away; the insatiable curiosity
and appetite for its continuation.
Emerson, E, II, 318.

NOTHING can be meaner than the anxiety to live on, to live on anyhow and in any shape; a spirit with any honour is not willing to live except in its own way, and a spirit with any wisdom is not over-eager to live at all.

Santayana, E, 164.

WHY should we have only two or three ways of life, and not thousands?

Emerson, J, VI, 491.

WHAT had I . . . to tell you? What, but that life was still tolerable; still absurdly sweet; still promising, promising, to credulous idleness.

Ibid., L, II, 217.

IV
THE AGE

It is long since the sick world began to doat and talk idly: would she had but doated still!

Ben Jonson, 394.

'Tis too late to be ambitious. The great mutations of the world are acted, or time may be too short for our designs.

Sir Thomas Browne, U, 26.

In this Age, when it is said of a Man, He knows *how to live*, it may be implied he is not very honest.

Halifax, 232.

Wheresoever manners and fashions are corrupted, language is. It imitates the public riot.

Ben Jonson, 402.

This Age will serve to make a very pretty Farce for the next, if it have any Wit at all to make Use of it.

Samuel Butler, Author of Hudibras, 475.

The world always had the same bankrupt look, to foregoing ages as to us,—as of a failed world just recollecting its old withered forces to begin again and try to do a little business.

Emerson, E, IV, 177.

What age was not dull? When were not the majority wicked? or what progress was ever made by society? Society is always flat and foolish.

Ibid., J, IV, 85.

Every Age, like every human body, has its own distemper.

Ibid., E, III, 481.

OUR age is retrospective. It builds the sepulchres of
the fathers. It writes biographies, histories and
criticism. The foregoing generations beheld God and
nature face to face; we, through their eyes.

Emerson, E, II, 371.

I CANNOT think Nature is so spent and decayed, that
she can bring forth nothing worth her former years.
. Men are decayed, and studies: she is not.

Ben Jonson, 391.

WE think our civilization near its meridian, but we
are yet only at the cock-crowing and the morning star.

Emerson, E, I, 316.

THE obscurest epoch is to-day.

R. L. Stevenson, E, 113.

V

MAN

WHAT a piece of work is a man!   How noble in reason!
How infinite in faculty!   In form, in moving, how
express and admirable!   In action how like an angel!
In apprehension how like a god!   The beauty of the
world!   The paragon of animals!   And yet, to me,
what is this quintessence of dust?

Hamlet, II, ii.

THE world to me is but a dream, or mock-show, and
we all therein but Pantaloons and Antics to my severer
contemplations.

Sir Thomas Browne, R, 88.

MAN is a noble Animal, splendid in ashes, and pompous
in the grave, solemnizing Nativities and Deaths with
equal lustre, nor omitting Ceremonies of bravery, in
the infamy of his nature.   *Ibid., U*, 29.

MANKIND is a tribe of animals, living by habits and
thinking in symbols; and it can never be anything else.

Santayana, V.

MAN, biologically considered, . . . is the most formidable of all beasts of prey, and, indeed, the only one that
preys systematically on its own species.

Wm. James, Memories and Studies, 301.

THERE is all Africa, and her prodigies in us.

Sir Thomas Browne, R, 30.

I KNOW, by not knowing even myself, how little I
know of that good, that bad, that knowing, that ignorant, that reasoning and unreasonable creature, Man.

Chesterfield, 1411

Man is the only animal that laughs and weeps; for he is the only animal that is struck with the difference between what things are, and what they ought to be.

Hazlitt, E C, 1.

We are the creatures of imagination, passion and self-will, more than of reason or even of self-interest . . . Even in the common transactions and daily intercourse of life, we are governed by whim, caprice, prejudice, or accident. The falling of a teacup puts us out of temper for the day; and a quarrel that commenced about the pattern of a gown may end only with our lives.

Ibid., W, XI, 259.

Man is a *make-believe* animal—he is never so truly himself as when he is acting a part.

Ibid., J, 246.

Man is an intellectual animal, and therefore an ever-lasting contradiction to himself. His senses centre in himself, his ideas reach to the ends of the universe; so that he is torn in pieces between the two, without a possibility of its ever being otherwise.

Ibid., C, 63.

Mankind are an incorrigible race. Give them but bugbears and idols—it is all that they ask.

Ibid., W, XI, 557.

It is hard for a pure and thoughtful man to live in a state of rapture at the spectacle afforded him by his fellow-creatures.   *Matthew Arnold,* 436.

It is not by sitting still at a grand distance and calling the human race *larvae,* that men are to be helped.

Emerson, E, IV, 174.

LET us treat the men and women well: treat them as if they were real: perhaps they are.

Emerson, E, I, 231.

IN brief, we are all monsters, that is, a composition of man and beast.

Sir Thomas Browne, R, 118.

I WONDER what pleasure men can take in making beasts of themselves!

I wonder, Madam, that you have not penetration enough to see the strong inducement to this excess; for he who makes a *beast* of himself gets rid of the pain of being a man.

Dr. Johnson, H, 144.

THE busy part of mankind will furnish the contemplative with the materials of speculation to the end of time.

Ibid., W, IX, 82.

FOR though the most be players, some must be spectators.

Ben Jonson, 404.

VI

REASON

A Man that doth not use his Reason, is a tame Beast; a Man that abuses it, is a wild one.

Halifax, 254.

Truth is man's proper good; and the only immortal thing was given to our mortality to use.

Ben Jonson, 397.

The mind of man is far from the nature of a clear and equal glass, . . . nay, it is rather like an enchanted glass, full of superstition and imposture.

Bacon, A, 200.

Where Sense is wanting, everything is wanting.

Halifax, 248.

A rush of thoughts is the only conceivable prosperity that can come to us.

Emerson, E, III, 324.

The mind celebrates a little triumph whenever it can formulate a truth.

Santayana, R, IV, 65.

Such is the delight of mental superiority, that none on whom nature or study have conferred it, would purchase the gifts of fortune by its loss.

Dr. Johnson, R, No. 150.

It takes a great deal of elevation of thought to produce a very little elevation of life.

Emerson, J, IV, 441.

One thought fills immensity.

Blake.

WHAT is now proved was once only imagined.
Blake.

EVERY man seeks for truth; but God only knows who has found it.
Chesterfield, 58.

IGNORANCE is not so damnable as humbug, but when it prescribes pills it may happen to do more harm.
George Eliot, Felix Holt.

TRUTH . . . never comes into the World, but like a Bastard, to the ignominy of him that brought her forth.
Milton, I, 276.

THE new statement is always hated by the old, and to those dwelling in the old, comes like an abyss of scepticism.
Emerson, E, I, 163.

'TIS real Humanity and Kindness, to hide strong Truths from tender Eyes.
Shaftesbury, I, 63.

GOD screens men from premature ideas.
Emerson, J, IV, 126.

ONE of the greatest pains to human nature is the pain of a new idea.
Bagehot, P, 163.

NOTHING hath an uglier Look to us than Reason, when it is not of our side.
Halifax, 254.

IN an unreasonable Age, a Man's Reason let loose would undo him.
Ibid., 246.

A Man may dwell so long upon a Thought, that it may take him Prisoner.

Halifax, 249.

A favourite theory is a possession for life.

Hazlitt, C, 52.

The wise only possess ideas; the greater part of mankind are possessed by them.

Coleridge, M, 154.

We think as we do, mainly because other people think so. *Samuel Butler, N,* 328.

Happy those who are convinced so as to be of the general Opinions.

Halifax, 227.

A great English divine has been described as always leaving out the principle upon which his arguments rested; even if it was stated to him, he regarded it as far-fetched and extravagant.

Bagehot, B, 193.

Whatever withdraws us from the power of our senses; whatever makes the past, the distant, or the future predominate over the present, advances us in the dignity of thinking beings.

Dr. Johnson, W, X, 501.

The dull pray; the geniuses are light mockers. How respectable is earnestness on every platform! but intellect kills it.

Emerson, E, I, 450.

All true knowledge contradicts common sense.

Bishop Creighton, L.

BY nature's kindly disposition most questions which it is beyond a man's power to answer do not occur to him at all.

Santayana, V.

A MAN doubtful of his dinner, or trembling at a creditor, is not much disposed to abstracted meditation, or remote inquiries.

Dr. Johnson, W, IV, 205.

METAPHYSICS is the finding of bad reasons for what we believe upon instinct; but to find these reasons is no less an instinct.

F. H. Bradley, XIV.

TRUTH is the object of philosophy, but not always of philosophers.

Churton Collins, E, 102.

A SYSTEM-GRINDER hates the truth.

Emerson, J, III, 523.

WHEN speculation has done its worst, two and two still make four.

Dr. Johnson, Idler, No. 36.

WHAT have you to do with Liberty and Necessity? Or what more than to hold your tongue about it?

Ibid., B, IV, 71.

I HATE to be near the sea, and to hear it roaring and raging like a wild beast in its den. It puts me in mind of the everlasting efforts of the human mind, struggling to be free, and ending just where it began.

Hazlitt, W, XI, 550.

7 1

VII

PREJUDICE

PREJUDICE is never easy unless it can pass itself off for reason.

Hazlitt, S E, 90.

OUR prejudices are our mistresses; reason is at best our wife, very often heard indeed, but seldom minded.

Chesterfield, 511.

No wise man can have a contempt for the prejudices of others; and he should even stand in a certain awe of his own, as if they were aged parents and monitors. They may in the end prove wiser than he.

Hazlitt, C, 55.

WITHOUT the aid of prejudice and custom, I should not be able to find my way across the room.

Ibid., S E, 98.

VIII

MEMORY

ALMOST twenty years since, I heard a profane jest, and still remember it. How many pious passages of a far later date have I forgotten! It seems my soul is like a filthy pond, wherein fish die soon, and frogs live long.

Thomas Fuller, T, 84.

COULD we know what Men are most apt to remember, we might know what they are most apt to do.

Halifax, 252.

THE Memory will seldom be unmannerly but where it is unkind.

Ibid., 251.

METHOD is the Mother of Memory.

Thomas Fuller, W, 166.

THE true art of memory is the art of attention.

Dr. Johnson, Idler, No. 74.

THOSE who cannot remember the past are condemned to repeat it.

Santayana, R, I, 284.

GENIUS

When thou seest an Eagle, thou seest a portion of Genius; lift up thy head!   *Blake.*

The roaring of lions, the howling of wolves, the raging of the stormy sea, and the destructive sword, are portions of eternity, too great for the eye of man.

Ibid.

The cistern contains: the fountain overflows.   *Ibid.*

No bird soars too high, if he soars with his own wings.
Ibid.

The eagle never lost so much time as when he submitted to learn of the crow.   *Ibid.*

When a true genius appears in the world, you may know him by this sign, that the dunces are all in confederacy against him.   *Swift*, III, 395.

Genius is at first shy and taken up with itself. The new world of thought or enterprise that is forming in the imagination jostles against and repels the actual one.
Hazlitt, B, I, 380.

Great geniuses have the shortest biographies. Their cousins can tell you nothing about them.
Emerson, E, I, 378.

Genius and Virtue, like diamonds, are best plain set,— set in lead, set in poverty.   *Ibid., J*, V, 260.

Genius . . . has been defined as a supreme capacity for taking trouble . . . It might be more fitly described as a supreme capacity for getting its possessors into trouble of all kinds.   *Samuel Butler, N*, 174.

X

THE PASSIONS

THERE seem near as many people that want passion as want reason.

Shenstone, 256.

WE are not so much Masters of our Heat as to have enough to warm our Thoughts, and not so much as to set them on fire.

Halifax, 246.

WISE people may say what they will, but one passion is never cured but by another.

Chesterfield, 1065.

THO' thou canst not pull thy Passions out by the Roots, yet it's in thy Power to hold them down, for a Time at least.

Dr. Fuller, II, 29.

HUMAN character, however it may be exalted, or depressed, by a temporary enthusiasm, will return by degrees to its proper and natural level, and will resume those passions that seem the most adapted to its present condition. *Gibbon*, *H*, XV.

SENTIMENTS are for the most part traditional; we feel them because they were felt by those who preceded us.

Hazlitt, *B*, IV, 436.

CURIOSITY is, in great and generous minds, the first passion and the last.

Dr. Johnson, *R*, No. 150.

CURIOSITY is the direct incontinency of the spirit.

Jeremy Taylor, *L*, 129.

HOPE AND DESIRE

MOST Men let their Wishes run away with them. They have no Mind to stop them in their career, the Motion is so pleasing.

Halifax, 248.

MEN should do with their Hopes as they do with tame Fowl, cut their Wings that they may not fly over the Wall.

Ibid., 237.

HOPE is a kind Cheat: in the Minute of our Disappointment we are angry, but upon the whole matter there is no Pleasure without it.

Ibid., 236.

HOPE is generally a wrong Guide, though it is very good company by the way.

Ibid.

HOPES—the only tie which keeps the heart from breaking.

Thomas Fuller, *W*, I, 40.

HOPE is itself a species of happiness, and, perhaps, the chief happiness which this world affords.

Dr. Johnson, *B*, I, 368.

SOME desire is necessary to keep life in motion.

Ibid., *W*, XI, 23.

No sooner are we supplied with everything that nature can demand, than we sit down to contrive artificial appetites.

Ibid., *Idler*, No. 30.

I KNOW not anything more pleasant, or more instructive, than to compare experience with expectation,
or to register from time to time the difference between
idea and reality.

Dr. Johnson, B, I, 337.

TO-MORROW is an old deceiver, and his cheat never
grows stale.

Ibid., L, I, 221.

THERE is more pleasure in building castles in the air
than on the ground.

Gibbon, M, I, 278.

WE all live upon the hope of pleasing somebody.

Dr. Johnson, B, II, 22.

THE natural flights of the human mind are not from
pleasure to pleasure, but from hope to hope.

Ibid., R, No. 2.

XII

AMBITION

THOUGH ambition itself be a vice, it is often the cause of great virtue. Give me that wit whom praise excites, glory puts on, or disgrace grieves; he is to be nourished with ambition, pricked forward with honour, checked with reprehension, and never to be suspected of sloth.

Ben Jonson, 411.

HARDLY anything will bring a man's mind into full activity if ambition be wanting.

Sir Henry Taylor, S, 132.

WHERE there are large powers with little ambition . . nature may be said to have fallen short of her purposes.

Ibid.

FEW men deliberately conclude with themselves that happiness in life is to be best promoted by accomplishing the objects of ambition; and their better judgment notwithstanding, most men will make their election of those objects. Do they not then desire to be happy? . . . The true answer is, that in such cases the thing desired and elected *is* for the *immediate* happiness of the party, and is contrary only to his happiness in the long run . . . It is thus that for the pleasure of the *transition* (which is a real pleasure so long as it lasts) we sacrifice the *state*.

Ibid., 133.

THE hope, and not the fact, of advancement, is the spur to industry.

Ibid., 187.

A CHIEF Thing which thou hast to study and endeavour in this World is, to make thy Life comfortable.

Dr. Fuller, II, 20.

A GREAT Reputation is a great Charge, very hard for a Man to acquit himself well of; I'll tell thee my very Thought: an obscure Life is more natural, the more easy.

Ibid., 57.

AMBITION sufficiently plagues her Proselytes, by keeping them always in Show and in Public, like a Statue in a street.

Ibid., 130.

NEVER desire and affect to be a governing, leading Man, in the Place thou livest in.

Ibid., 156.

HE that fails in his endeavours after wealth or power, will not long retain either honesty or courage.

Dr. Johnson, A, No. 99.

XIII

FAME, REPUTATION

THE highest form of vanity is love of fame. It is a passion easy to deride but hard to understand, and in men who live at all by imagination almost impossible to eradicate. *Santayana, E,* 22.

WE speak of fame as the reward of genius, whereas in truth genius, the imaginative dominion of experience, is its own reward, and fame is but a foolish image by which its worth is symbolized.

Ibid., R, II, 145.

THE desiring to be remember'd when we are dead, is to so little purpose, that it is fit Men should, as they generally are, be disappointed in it. Nevertheless, the desire of leaving a good Name behind us is so honourable to ourselves, and so useful to the World, that good Sense must not be heard against it.

Halifax, 241.

OF those who have thus survived themselves most completely, left a sort of personal seduction behind them in the world, and retained, after death, the art of making friends, Montaigne and Samuel Johnson certainly stand first.

R. L. Stevenson, B, 237.

PLINY leaves mankind this only alternative: either of doing what deserves to be written, or of writing what deserves to be read. *Chesterfield,* 275.

THE love of fame is almost another name for the love of excellence; or it is the ambition to attain the highest excellence, sanctioned by the highest authority, that of time. *Hazlitt, R T,* II, 58.

FAME is not popularity, the shout of the multitude,
. . it is the spirit of a man surviving himself in the
minds and thoughts of other men, undying and imperishable.   *Hazlitt, E P,* 283.

THE blaze of reputation cannot be blown out, but it
often dies in the socket; a very few names may be
considered as perpetual lamps that shine unconsumed.
                                    Dr. Johnson, B, III, 423.

WHAT forests of laurel we bring, and the tears of mankind, to those who stood firm against the opinion of
their contemporaries!
                                    Emerson, E, II, 277.

THERE are names written in her immortal scroll, at
which Fame blushes!   *Hazlitt, C,* 22.

MEN, and almost all sort of creatures, have their reputation by distance.   *Ben Jonson,* 408.

THE fame of a great man is not rigid and stony like his
bust.   It changes with time.   It needs time to give it
due perspective.
                                    Emerson, E, IV, 73.

ALL reputations each age revises.   Very few immut-
able men has History to show.
                                    Ibid., J, V, 312.

I AM more famed in Heaven for my works than I
could well conceive.

                                    Blake, L, I, 150.

ESTEEM to Virtue is like a cherishing Air to Plants and
Flowers, which maketh them blow and prosper.
                                    Halifax, 43.

THE invisible Thing called a Good Name, is made up of the Breath of Numbers that speak well of you.

Halifax, 37.

PRAISES of the unworthy are felt by ardent minds as robberies of the deserving.

Coleridge, B, Chap. III.

EITHER a good or a bad reputation outruns and gets before people wherever they go.

Chesterfield, 902.

THE highest panegyric . . . that private virtue can receive is the praise of servants.

Dr. Johnson, R, No. 68.

IT is reasonable to rejoice, as the day declines, to find that it has been spent with the approbation of mankind.

Ibid., L, II, 369.

CONTEMPT is a kind of gangrene, which if it seizes one part of a character corrupts all the rest.

Ibid., W, III, 186.

AH! Sir, a boy being flogged is not so severe as a man having the hiss of the world against him.

Ibid., B, I, 451.

WHAT is ill fame, but a little corrupted unsavoury Breath?

Dr. Fuller, II, 147.

THE Man that despiseth Slander deserveth it.

Halifax, 255.

THE Contempt of good Reputation is called Impudence.

Hobbes, 27.

XIV

EGOTISM

EVERY man is of importance to himself.
Dr. Johnson, W, IV, 53.

THERE is none almost who has not this misleading egotism. The efficient men are efficient by means of this Flanders horse.
Emerson, J, X, 18.

TAKE egotism out, and you would castrate the benefactors.
Ibid., IX, 519.

MOST men are afflicted with a coldness, an incuriosity, as soon as any object does not connect with their self-love. Though they talk of the object before them, they are thinking of themselves, and their vanity is laying little traps for your admiration.
Ibid., E, II, 260.

SELFISHNESS is calm, a force of nature: you might say the trees were selfish.
R. L. Stevenson, E, 83.

INTOLERANCE itself is a form of egoism, and to condemn egoism intolerantly is to share it.
Santayana, W, 151.

I MUST complain the cards are ill-shuffled, till I have a good hand.
Swift, XI, 322.

To love oneself is the beginning of a lifelong romance.
Oscar Wilde, 49.

I AM God in nature; I am a weed by the wall.
Emerson, E, I, 164

No man is much regarded by the rest of the world. He that considers how little he dwells upon the condition of others, will learn how little the attention of others is attracted by himself. While we see multitudes passing before us, of whom perhaps not one appears to deserve our notice or excite our sympathy, we should remember, that we likewise are lost in the same throng; that the eye which happens to glance upon us is turned in a moment on him that follows us, and that the utmost which we can reasonably hope or fear, is to fill a vacant hour with prattle, and be forgotten.
Dr. Johnson, R, No. 159.

XV

SELF-KNOWLEDGE

As accidental as my Life may be, or as that random Humour is, which governs it; I know nothing, after all, so real or substantial as Myself.

Shaftesbury, II, 353.

IF we would really know our heart, let us impartially view our actions.

Bishop Wilson, M, 151.

VERY few can boast of hearts which they dare lay open to themselves, and of which, by whatever accident exposed, they do not shun a distinct and continued view.

Dr. Johnson, W, IV, 96.

WE can hardly be confident of the state of our own minds, but as it stands attested by some external action; we are seldom sure that we sincerely meant what we omitted to do.

Ibid., L, I, 353.

A MAN finds he has been wrong at every preceding stage of his career, only to deduce the astonishing conclusion that he is at last entirely right.

R. L. Stevenson, V, 104.

WE never despise others, but when we do not reflect upon ourselves.

Bishop Wilson, M, 57.

SELF-LOVE is often rather arrogant than blind; it does not hide our faults from ourselves, but persuades us that they escape the notice of others.

Dr. Johnson, R, No. 155.

NOTHING softeneth the Arrogance of our Nature, like a Mixture of some Frailties. It is by them that we are best told, that we must not strike too hard upon

85

others, because we ourselves do so often deserve Blows. They pull our Rage by the Sleeve, and whisper Gentleness to us in our Censures. *Halifax*, 12.

WE meet people who seem to overlook and read us with a smile, but they do not tell us what they read.
Emerson, *J*, X, 304.

NOTHING requires a rarer intellectual heroism than willingness to see one's equation written out.
Santayana, *E*, 37.

HUMILITY is a virtue all men preach, none practise, and yet everybody is content to hear. The Master thinks it good Doctrine for his Servants, the Laity for the Clergy, and the Clergy for the Laity. *Selden*, 53.

THE most useful Part of Wisdom is for a Man to give a good guess, what others think of him.

It is a dangerous thing to guess partially, and a melancholy thing to guess right.

Halifax, 255.

WE are all apt to believe what the world believes about us. *George Eliot, Mill on the Floss.*

THE men who can be charged with fewest failings . . . are generally most ready to allow them.
Dr. Johnson, *R*, No. 31.

I KNOW myself (no common piece of knowledge, let me tell you), I know what I can, what I cannot, and consequently what I ought to do.

Chesterfield, 608.

PERHAPS the only true dignity of man is his capacity to despise himself. *Santayana*, *E*, 230.

XVI

VIRTUE AND VICE

Virtue is like hunger or thirst; it must be satisfied or we die.

Jeremy Taylor, S, II, 189.

If goodness were only a theory, it were a pity it should be lost to the world. There are a number of things, the idea of which is a clear gain to the mind. Let people, for instance, rail at friendship, genius, freedom, as long as they will—the very names of these despised qualities are better than anything else that could be substituted for them, and embalm even the most envenomed satire against them.

Hazlitt, S E, 40.

He can never be good that is not obstinate.

Bishop Wilson, M, 126.

Tread softly and circumspectly in this funambulatory track and narrow path of goodness.

Sir Thomas Browne, C, 7.

It is the mark of a good action that it appears inevitable in the retrospect.

R. L. Stevenson, E, 84.

Habits are the daughters of action, but then they nurse their mother, and produce daughters after her image, but far more beautiful and prosperous.

Jeremy Taylor, S, I, 181.

A man who only does what every one of the society to which he belongs would do, is not a dishonest man.

Dr. Johnson, B, II, 176.

CONSCIENCE is, in most men, an anticipation of the opinion of others.

Sir Henry Taylor, S, 63.

THERE is another man within me that's angry with me.
Sir Thomas Browne, R, 148.

THE conscience has morbid sensibilities; it must be employed but not indulged, like the imagination or the stomach.

R. L. Stevenson, E, 84.

IF your morals make you dreary, depend upon it they are wrong.

Ibid., 70.

THE greatest burden in the World is Superstition, not only of Ceremonies in the Church, but of imaginary and scarecrow Sins at home.

Milton, I, 277.

THE exactest vigilance and caution can never maintain a single day of unmingled innocence.

Dr. Johnson, R, No. 14.

WHERE there is yet shame, there may in time be virtue.
Ibid., W, X, 319.

A vow is a horrible thing, it is a snare for sin.
Ibid., B, III, 357.

REMEMBER that you are something more than body.
Bishop Wilson, M, 147.

MAN'S chief merit consists in resisting the impulses of his nature.

Dr. Johnson, M, II, 285.

HE that strives against nature, will for ever strive in vain.

Dr. Johnson, Idler, No. 51.

SOONER murder an infant in its cradle than nurse un-acted desires.

Blake.

A MORTIFIED appetite is never a wise companion.

R. L. Stevenson, E, 69.

THE road of excess leads to the palace of wisdom.

Blake.

WHEN we see a soul whose acts are all regal, graceful, and pleasant as roses, we must thank God that such things can be and are, and not turn sourly on the angel, and say, "Crump is a better man with his grunting resistance to all his native devils."

Emerson, E, I, 71.

NOTHING is more unpleasant than a virtuous person with a mean mind.

Bagehot, L, II, 373.

I AM not mortified by our vice, . . but, I own our virtue makes me ashamed.

Emerson, E, III, 480.

IT is easier to make a saint out of a libertine than out of a prig.

Santayana, E, 253.

IT is good to be without vices, but it is not good to be without temptations.

Bagehot, B, 237.

NATURE is innocent, and so are all her impulses and moods when taken in isolation; it is only on meeting that they blush. *Santayana, E,* 247.

THE devil never tempts us with more success, than when he tempts us with a sight of our own good actions.
Bishop Wilson, M, 115.

HE that fancies he is perfect, may lose that by pride which he attained by grace.
Ibid., 108.

VIRTUE is too often merely local.
Dr. Johnson, Idler, No. 53.

So much are the modes of excellence settled by time and place, that men may be heard boasting in one street of that which they would anxiously conceal in another.
Ibid., R, No. 201.

As every man prefers virtue, when there is not some strong incitement to transgress its precepts, I can conceive him doing nothing wrong. But if such a man stood in need of money, I should not like to trust him; and I should certainly not trust him with young ladies, for *there* there is always temptation.
Ibid., B, I, 444.

No man practises so well as he writes. I have, all my life long, been lying till noon; yet I tell all young men, and tell them with great sincerity, that nobody who does not rise early will ever do any good.
Ibid., V, 210.

THE mind is enlarged and elevated by mere purposes, though they end as they begin by airy contemplation. We compare and judge, though we do not practise.

Dr. Johnson, L, II, 361.

WE do what we must, and call it by the best names.

Emerson, E, II, 322.

THE vices we scoff at in others, laugh at us within ourselves.

Sir Thomas Browne, C, 110.

THERE is a division of labour, even in vice. Some persons addict themselves to the speculation only, others to the practice.

Hazlitt, D, 144.

THE vices are never so well employed as in combating one another.

Ibid., Sh, 39.

MANY might go to heaven with half the labour they go to hell.

Ben Jonson, 392.

THE virtues of society are vices of the saint.

Emerson, E, I, 170.

THAT can never be good for the bee which is bad for the swarm.

Ibid., IV, 385.

IT is easy to live for others; everybody does.

Ibid., J, VII, 46.

SELF-SACRIFICE enables us to sacrifice other people without blushing.

Bernard Shaw, 244.

EVERY hero becomes a bore at last.

Emerson, E, I, 370.

A COLD, and cynical wisdom particularly disapproves of most men's *best* actions.

Bagehot, B, 264.

IF people had no vices but their own, few would have so many as they have. For my own part, I would sooner wear other people's clothes than their vices; and they would sit upon me just as well.

Chesterfield, 208.

SINS in the regenerate are only the breaking forth of leaves in the trunk that is felled.

Coventry Patmore, 75.

WHERE a good life is lived, it hardly becomes us to be too critical of motives and springs of action.

Mackail, L, 227.

THE frontiers between sense and spirit are the devil's hunting-grounds

Coventry Patmore, 70.

THE heart of man is the place the Devils dwell in: I feel sometimes a Hell within myself, Lucifer keeps his Court in my breast, Legion is revived in me.

Sir Thomas Browne, R, 111.

HE that will not command his thoughts . . . will soon lose the command of his actions.

Bishop Wilson, S, 153.

OUR thoughts are often worse than we are.

George Eliot, Mr. Gilfil's Love Story.

WE are no more responsible for the evil thoughts which pass through our minds, than a scarecrow for the birds which fly over the seed-plot he has to guard; the sole responsibility in each case is to prevent them from settling.

Churton Collins, E, 97.

WE love to overlook the boundaries which we do not wish to pass.

Dr. Johnson, R, No. 114.

THAT which we call sin in others, is experiment for us.

Emerson, E, I, 241.

No evil is pure, nor hell itself without its extreme satisfactions.

Ibid., 171.

ONE does not begin to fall when the fall becomes sensible.

Bishop Wilson, M, 115.

OUR faith comes in moments; our vice is habitual.

Emerson, E, I, 143.

FOR how many years did Mr. Pepys continue to make and break his little vows? And yet I have not heard that he was discouraged in the end.

R. L. Stevenson, V, 28.

XVII

PLEASURE

Pleasures are all alike simply considered in themselves; he that hunts or he that governs the Commonwealth, they both please themselves alike, only we commend that, whereby we ourselves receive some benefit.

Selden, 94.

Whilst ye are upon Earth, Enjoy the good things that are here (to that end were they given) and be not Melancholy, and wish yourself in heaven.

Ibid.

'Tis a wrong way to proportion other men's pleasures to ourselves; 'tis like a Child's using a little bird, O poor bird thou shalt sleep with me; so lays it in his Bosom and stifles it with his hot breath; the bird had rather be in the cold air.

Ibid.

Is there that sordid Creature on earth, who does not prize his own Enjoyment?

Shaftesbury, II, 228.

Life admits not of delays; when pleasure can be had, it is fit to catch it.

Dr. Johnson, B, III, 131.

Enjoy every moment; pleasures do not commonly last so long as life.

Chesterfield, 528.

Few men can be men of pleasure, every man may be a rake.

Ibid., 370.

IN our present state of existence, the body is so inseparably connected with the soul, that it seems to be our interest to taste, with innocence and moderation, the enjoyments of which that faithful companion is susceptible.

Gibbon, H, XV.

LIFE must be filled up, and the man who is not capable of intellectual pleasures must content himself with such as his senses can afford.

Dr. Johnson, M, I, 251.

THE race of delight is short, and pleasures have mutable faces.

Sir Thomas Browne, C, 53.

LIFE is a progress from want to want, not from enjoyment to enjoyment.

Dr. Johnson, B, III, 53.

IF pleasure was not followed by pain, who would forbear it?

Ibid., Idler, No. 89.

AMUSEMENT is the happiness of those that cannot think.

Pope, 304.

NOTHING is more hopeless than a scheme of merriment.
Dr. Johnson, Idler, No. 58.

THE public pleasures of far the greater part of mankind are counterfeit.

Ibid., No. 18.

IT is easy to talk of sitting at home contented, when others are seeing or making shows. But not to have been where it is supposed, and seldom supposed falsely, that all would go if they could; to be able to say nothing when everyone is talking; to have no opinion when everyone is judging; to hear exclamations of rapture without power to depress; to listen to falsehoods without right to contradict, is, after all, a state of temporary inferiority, in which the mind is rather hardened by stubbornness, than supported by fortitude . . . You that have seen the regatta will have images which we who miss it must want, and no intellectual images are without use.

Dr. Johnson, L, I, 337.

THAT the regatta disappointed you is neither wonderful nor new; all pleasure preconceived and preconcerted ends in disappointment; but disappointment, when it involves neither shame nor loss, is as good as success; for it supplies as many images to the mind, and as many topics to the tongue.

Ibid., 339.

OUR intercourse with the dead is better than our intercourse with the living. There are only three pleasures in life pure and lasting, and all derived from inanimate things—books, pictures, and the face of nature.

Hazlitt, A, I, 40.

IF I had no duties, and no reference to futurity, I would spend my life in driving briskly in a post-chaise with a pretty woman.

Dr. Johnson, B, III, 162.

96

IT is very strange, and very melancholy, that the paucity of human pleasures should persuade us ever to call hunting one of them.

Dr. Johnson, M, I, 288.

THE great pleasure in life is doing what people say you cannot do.

Bagehot, L, I, 171.

THERE is a pleasure in madness, which none but madmen know. *Hazlitt, D, 346.*

SIMPLE pleasures . . . are the last refuge of the complex.

Oscar Wilde, 35.

A LIFE of pleasure requires an aristocratic setting to make it interesting or really conceivable.

Santayana, R, II, 135.

THERE is something artificial in the deliberate pursuit of pleasure . . .   The sad business of life is rather to escape certain dreadful evils to which our nature exposes us,—death, hunger, disease, weariness, isolation, and contempt.   By the awful authority of these things, which stand like spectres behind every moral injunction, conscience in reality speaks, and a mind which they have duly impressed cannot but feel, by contrast, the hopeless triviality of the search for pleasure.

Ibid., E, 249.

BUSINESS is really more agreeable than pleasure; it interests the whole mind, the aggregate nature of man more continuously, and more deeply.   But it does not *look* as if it did.

Bagehot, E, 117.

XVIII

HAPPINESS

THERE is nothing, Sir, too little for so little a creature
as man. It is by studying little things that we attain
the great art of having as little misery and as much
happiness as possible.

Dr. Johnson, B, I, 433.

OUR brightest blazes of gladness are commonly kindled
by unexpected sparks.

Ibid., Idler, No. 58.

HAPPINESS consists in the multiplicity of agreeable
consciousness. *Ibid., B,* II, 9.

THE happiest part of a man's life is what he passes
lying awake in bed in the morning.
("I may perhaps have said this; for nobody, at times,
talks more laxly than I do.")

Ibid., V, 352.

SIR, you observed one day at General Oglethorpe's,
that a man is never happy for the present, but when
he is drunk. Will you not add,—or when driving
rapidly in a post-chaise?
No, Sir, you are driving rapidly *from* something, or
to something.

Ibid., III, 5.

VERY few men, properly speaking, live at present, but
are providing to live another time.

Swift, III, 411.

WHAT is climate to happiness? Place me in the heart
of Asia, should I not be exiled? What proportion does
climate bear to the complex system of human life?

You may advise me to go to live at Bologna to eat sausages. The sausages there are the best in the world: they lose much by being carried.

Dr. Johnson, B, II, 195.

To enjoy true happiness, we must travel into a very far country, and even out of ourselves.

Sir Thomas Browne, C, 101.

Sir, when a man is tired of London, he is tired of life; for there is in London all that life can afford.

Dr. Johnson, B, III, 178.

Why, Sir, Fleet Street has a very animated appearance; but, I think the full tide of human existence is at Charing Cross.

Ibid., II, 337.

Sir, there is nothing which has yet been contrived by man by which so much happiness is produced as by a good tavern or inn.

Ibid., 452.

As soon as I enter the door of a tavern, I experience an oblivion of care, and a freedom from solicitude: when I am seated, I find the master courteous, and the servants obsequious to my call; anxious to know and ready to supply my wants; wine there exhilarates my spirits, and prompts me to free conversation and an interchange of discourse with those whom I most love: I dogmatize and am contradicted, and in this conflict of opinions and sentiments I find delight.

Ibid., M, II, 91.

But man is not born for happiness.

Ibid., W, IV, 206.

THAT kind of life is most happy which affords us most opportunities of gaining our own esteem.

Dr. Johnson, W IX, 114.

ENERGY is Eternal Delight.

Blake.

THE soul of sweet delight can never be defiled.

Ibid.

WEAK is the joy which is never wearied.

Ibid., L, I, 62.

GOOD temper is an estate for life.

Hazlitt, P S, II, 106.

WHATEVER surly sweetness possession can give, is tasted in England to the dregs.

Emerson, E, II, 96.

How does nature deify us with a few and cheap elements! Give me health and a day, and I will make the pomp of emperors ridiculous.

Ibid., 379.

THE Negro, thanks to his temperament, appears to make the greatest amount of happiness out of the smallest capital.

Ibid., J, X, 176.

THE fewer desires, the more peace.

Bishop Wilson, M, 27.

HAPPINESS is something men ought to pursue, although they seldom do so.

Santayana, E, 119.

HAPPINESS

HAPPINESS is the only sanction of life; where happiness fails, existence remains a mad and lamentable experiment.

Santayana, E, 251.

THE measure of a happy Life is not from the fewer or more Suns we behold, the fewer or more Breaths we draw, or Meals we repeat; but from the having once lived well, acted our Part handsomely, and made our Exit cheerfully, and as became us.

Shaftesbury, I, 316.

THERE is no duty we so much underrate as the duty of being happy.

R. L. Stevenson, V, 122.

XIX

MISFORTUNE, SORROW

Ill Fortune never crushed that man, whom good Fortune deceived not.

Ben Jonson, 390.

A Man must stoop sometimes to his ill Star, but he must never lie down to it.

Halifax, 238.

Complaining is a Contempt upon one's self:

It is an ill Sign both of a man's Head and of his Heart.

A Man throweth himself down whilst he complaineth; and when a Man throweth himself down, nobody careth to take him up again.

Ibid., 248.

The man that is once hated, both his good, and his evil deeds oppress him.

Ben Jonson, 390.

The world will never be long without some good reason to hate the unhappy.

Dr. Johnson, *A*, No. 99.

To tell of disappointment and misery, to thicken the darkness of futurity, and perplex the labyrinth of uncertainty, has been always a delicious employment of the poets.

Ibid., *W*, IV, 110.

The miseries of life would be increased beyond all human power of endurance, if we were to enter the world with the same opinions as we carry from it.

Ibid., *R*, No. 196.

He that wanders about the world sees new forms of human misery, and if he chances to meet an old friend, meets a face darkened with troubles.

Dr. Johnson, L, I, 227.

Where is the bottom of the misery of man?

Ibid., Idler, No. 41.

Sorrow is never long without a dawn of ease.

Ibid., W, XI, 99.

Afflictions induce callosities, miseries are slippery, or fall like snow upon us.

Sir Thomas Browne, U, 28.

Stay but till to-morrow, and your present sorrow will be weary, and will lie down to rest.

Jeremy Taylor, S, I, 327.

There is no wisdom in useless and hopeless sorrow; but there is something in it so like virtue, that he who is wholly without it cannot be loved.

Dr. Johnson, L, II, 215.

The saddest tragedy in the world is the destruction of what has within it no inward ground of dissolution, death in youth, and the crushing out of perfection.

Santayana, R, IV, 200.

To grieve for evils is often wrong; but it is much more wrong to grieve without them.

Dr. Johnson, L, II, 71.

If we murmur here, we may at the next melancholy be troubled that God did not make us to be Angels, or Stars. *Jeremy Taylor, L,* 138.

THERE is a Melancholy which accompanies all Enthusiasm.

Shaftesbury, I, 13.

MELANCHOLY, indeed, should be diverted by every means but drinking.

Dr. Johnson, B, III, 5.

SORROW is a kind of rust of the soul, which every new idea contributes in its passage to scour away.

Ibid., R, No. 47.

To know how just a cause we have for grieving is already a consolation, for it is already a shift from feeling to understanding.

Santayana, R, IV, 64.

To understand oneself is the classic form of consolation; to elude oneself is the romantic.

Ibid., W, 200.

GRIEF is a species of idleness.

Dr. Johnson, L, I, 212.

THE wretched have no compassion.

Ibid., II, 215.

ONE way of getting an idea of our fellow-countrymen's miseries is to go and look at their pleasures.

George Eliot, Felix Holt.

NEVER pity people because they are ill-used. They only wait the opportunity to use others just as ill.

Hazlitt, W, XII, 375.

THE busy bee has no time for sorrow.

Blake.

MISFORTUNE, SORROW

Joys impregnate. Sorrows bring forth.

Blake.

In general, the greatest reverses of fortune are the most easily borne from a sort of dignity belonging to them

Hazlitt, B, IV, 267.

There are people who have an appetite for grief, pleasure is not strong enough and they crave pain.

Emerson, E, IV, 191.

Our moods do not believe in each other.

Ibid., I, 164.

XX

HEALTH AND DISEASE

MEN that look no further than their outsides, think health an appurtenance unto life, and quarrel with their constitutions for being sick; but I that have examined the parts of man, and know upon what tender filaments that Fabric hangs, do wonder that we are not always so; and considering the thousand doors that lead to death, do thank my God that we can die but once.

Sir Thomas Browne, R, 93.

PHYSICAL ills are the taxes laid upon this wretched life; some are taxed higher, and some lower, but all pay something. *Chesterfield,* 1192.

DISEASE generally begins that equality which death completes. *Dr. Johnson, R,* No. 48.

WHAT can a sick man say, but that he is sick?
Ibid., B, IV, 362.

IT is so very difficult for a sick man not to be a scoundrel. *Ibid., M,* I, 267.

THE "madness of superfluous health" I have never known. *Gibbon, M,* I, 183.

IT is dainty to be sick, if you have leisure and convenience for it. *Emerson, J,* V, 162.

A PERSON seldom falls sick, but the bystanders are animated with a faint hope that he will die.
Ibid., E, II, 323.

WE all labour against our own cure, for death is the cure of all diseases.

Sir Thomas Browne, R, 159.

XXI

EATING AND DRINKING

SOME people have a foolish way of not minding, or of pretending not to mind, what they eat. For my part, I mind my belly very studiously and very carefully; for I look upon it that he who does not mind his belly will hardly mind anything else.

Dr. Johnson, B, I, 467.

A MAN seldom thinks with more earnestness of anything than he does of his dinner.

Ibid., M, I, 249.

SIR, when a man is invited to dinner, he is disappointed if he does not get something good.

Ibid., B, III, 186.

SOME hold, when hospitality died in England, she gave her last groan amongst the yeomen of Kent.

Thomas Fuller, H, 106.

A MAN who rides out for an appetite consults but little the dignity of human nature.

Dr. Johnson, H, 9.

I CAN reason down or deny everything, except this perpetual Belly: feed he must and will, and I cannot make him respectable.

Emerson, E, I, 452.

ANY of us would kill a cow rather than not have beef.

Dr. Johnson, B, V, 247.

MEN of great abilities are generally of a large and vigorous animal nature.

Sir Henry Taylor, S, 229.

IF thou farest well, enjoy it to thyself, and do not cry Roast-meat.

Dr. Fuller, II, 44.

DRINKING may be practised with great prudence; a man who exposes himself when he is intoxicated, has not the art of getting drunk.

Dr. Johnson, B, III, 389.

THERE are some sluggish men who are improved by drinking; as there are fruits which are not good till they are rotten.

Ibid., 42

SIR, I do not say it is wrong to produce self-complacency by drinking; I only deny that it improves the mind.

Ibid.

To make a man pleased with himself, let me tell you, is doing a very great thing.

Ibid., 328.

SIR, claret is the liquor for boys; port for men; but he who aspires to be a hero must drink brandy.

Ibid., 381.

GLORY not in making others drunk.

Dr. Fuller, II, 22

XXII

YOUTH AND AGE

YOUTH enters the world with very happy prejudices in her own favour.

> *Dr. Johnson, R,* No. 127.

IT is a state of continual ebriety for six or seven years at least, and frequently attended by fatal and permanent consequences, both to body and mind.

> *Chesterfield,* 652.

YOUNG men are as apt to think themselves wise enough, as drunken men are to think themselves sober enough. They look upon spirit to be a much better thing than experience, which they call coldness. They are but half-mistaken; for though spirit without experience is dangerous, experience, without spirit, is languid and defective.

> *Ibid.,* 569.

FOR God's sake give me the young man who has brains enough to make a fool of himself!

> *R. L. Stevenson, V,* 103.

SIR, I love the acquaintance of young people; because, in the first place, I don't like to think myself growing old. In the next place, young acquaintances must last longest, if they do last; and then, Sir, young men have more virtue than old men; they have more generous sentiments in every respect.

> *Dr. Johnson, B,* I, 445.

THE young man who intends no ill, believes that none is intended, and therefore acts with openness and candour; but his father, having suffered the injuries of fraud, is impelled to suspect, and too often allured to practise it.

> *Ibid., W,* XI, 72.

EVERY man over forty is a scoundrel.

Bernard Shaw, 242.

WHAT would you give, old gentleman, to be as young and sprightly as I am?

Why, Sir, I think I would almost be content to be as foolish.

Dr. Johnson, M, II, 69.

No wise man ever wished to be younger.

Swift, III, 402.

THE universities are a sort of lunatic asylum for keeping young men out of mischief.

Bishop Creighton.

I HOPE our young men will not grow into such *dodgers* as these old men are. I believe everything a *young* man says to me.

Jowett, 250.

A YOUNG man feels himself one too many in the world.

R. L. Stevenson, V, 150.

OLD men have in some degree their Reprisals upon younger, by making nicer Observations upon them.

Halifax, 256.

THE conversation of the old and young ends generally with contempt or pity on either side.

Dr. Johnson, R, No. 69.

AN old Man concludeth from his knowing Mankind, that they know him too, and that maketh him very wary.

Halifax, 246.

AGE stealeth so insensibly upon us, that we do not think of suiting our way of Reasoning to the several Stages of Life; so insensibly that not being able to pitch on any precise Time, when we cease to be young, we either flatter ourselves that we always continue to be so, or at least forget how much we are mistaken in it.

Halifax, 206.

THE return of my birthday, if I remember it, fills me with thoughts which it seems to be the general care of humanity to escape.

Dr. Johnson, B, V, 222.

To be interested in the changing seasons is, in this middling zone, a happier state of mind than to be hopelessly in love with spring.

Santayana, E, 277.

STATESMEN and beauties are very rarely sensible of the gradations of their decay; and, too sanguinely hoping to shine on in their meridian, often set with contempt and ridicule.

Chesterfield, 609.

THE heart never grows better by age; I fear rather worse, always harder. A young liar will be an old one, and a young knave will only be a greater knave as he grows older.

Ibid., 342.

TALKING is the disease of age.

Ben Jonson, 395.

WE grizzle every day. I see no need of it.

Emerson, E, I, 171.

AGE is rarely despised but when it is contemptible.
Dr. Johnson, R, No. 50.

DIGNITY, high station, or great riches, are in some
sort necessary to old men, to keep the younger at a
distance.
Swift, III, 407.

OLD men and comets have been reverenced for the
same reason: their long beards, and pretences to fore-
tell events.
Ibid., 409.

THERE is a wicked inclination in most people to suppose an old man decayed in his intellects. If a young
or middle-aged man, when leaving a company, does
not recollect where he laid his hat, it is nothing;
but if the same inattention is discovered in an old man,
people will shrug up their shoulders, and say "His
memory is going."
Dr. Johnson, B, IV, 181.

AT seventy-seven it is time to be earnest.
Ibid., B, V, 288.

IN the decline of life shame and grief are of short
duration.
Ibid., W, XI, 10.

AT every stage we lose a foe.
Emerson, E, III, 172.

FEW envy the consideration enjoyed by the oldest
inhabitant.
Ibid., 170.

OLD age brings along with its uglinesses the comfort that you will soon be out of it . . . . To be out of the war, out of debt, out of the drouth, out of the blues, out of the dentist's hands, out of the second thoughts, mortifications, and remorses that inflict such twinges and shooting pains,—out of the next winter, and the high prices, and the company below your ambition——
Emerson, J, X, 51.

XXIII

MONEY

MONEY makes a man laugh.

Selden, 100.

THERE are few ways in which a man can be more innocently employed than in getting money.

Dr. Johnson, B, II, 323.

GENERALLY Money lies nearest them that are nearest their Graves.

Wm. Penn, 151.

POWER pleases the violent and the proud; wealth delights the placid and the timorous. Youth therefore flies at power, and age grovels after riches.

Dr. Johnson, W, X, 431.

As an occupation in declining years, I declare I think saving is useful, amusing, and not unbecoming. It must be a perpetual amusement. It is a game that can be played by day, by night, at home and abroad, and at which you must win in the long run . . . . What an interest it imparts to life!

Thackeray, 251.

LIFE is short. The sooner that a man begins to enjoy his wealth the better.

Dr. Johnson, B, II, 226.

IF a man own land, the land owns him.

Emerson, E, II, 250.

MY cow milks me.

Ibid., J, V, 406.

THE price we have to pay for money is paid in liberty.

R. L. Stevenson, B, 138.

THEY who are of opinion that Money will do everything, may very well be suspected to do everything for Money.   *Halifax*, 242.

WHEN by habit a Man cometh to have a bargaining Soul, its Wings are cut, so that it can never soar.
                                        Ibid., 253.

COVETOUSNESS has such a blinding power that all the arguments in the world will not convince a man that he is covetous.
                              Bishop Wilson, M, 29.

THE poor work miracles every day: we give them, and they give us treasure in heaven.
                                        Ibid., 12.

GIVE nobly to indigent merit, and do not refuse your charity even to those who have no merit but their misery.
                                  Chesterfield, 657.

A PRINCELY MIND will undo a private Family.
                                      Halifax, 27.

IT is always so pleasant to be generous, though very vexatious to pay debts.
                                  Emerson, E, I, 285.

THOUGH Wisdom cannot be gotten for gold, still less can it be gotten without it. . . .   No gold, no Holy Ghost.
                              Samuel Butler, N, 172.

Do not discourage your children from hoarding, if they have a taste to it; whoever lays up his penny rather than part with it for a cake, at least is not the slave of gross appetite; and shows besides a preference always to be esteemed, of the future to the present moment.

Dr. Johnson, M, I, 251.

FEW listen without a desire of conviction to those who advise them to spare their money.

Ibid., Idler, No. 26.

SIR, all the arguments which are brought to represent poverty as no evil show it to be evidently a great evil. You never find people labouring to convince you that you may live very happily upon a plentiful fortune.

Ibid., B, I, 441.

POVERTY is a great enemy to human happiness; it certainly destroys liberty, and it makes some virtues impracticable, and other extremely difficult.

Ibid., IV, 157.

POVERTY is an anomaly to rich people. It is very difficult to make out why people who want dinner do not ring the bell.

Bagehot, L, II, 160.

SMALL debts are like small shot; they are rattling on every side, and can scarcely be escaped without a wound: great debts are like cannon; of loud noise, but little danger.

Dr. Johnson, B, I, 347.

MONEY and time are the heaviest burdens of life, and . . . the unhappiest of all mortals are those who have more of either than they know how to use.

Ibid., Idler, No. 30.

XXIV

IDLENESS

PERHAPS man is the only being that can properly be called idle.

Dr. Johnson, Idler, No. 1.

To do nothing is in every man's power; we can never want an opportunity of omitting duties.

Ibid., R, No. 155.

TIME, with all its celerity, moves slowly to him whose whole employment it is to watch its flight.

Ibid., Idler, No. 21.

THE idler never applauds his own idleness, nor does any man repent of the diligence of his youth.

Ibid., No. 94.

As peace is the end of war, so to be idle is the ultimate purpose of the busy.

Ibid., No. 1.

WE would all be idle if we could.

Ibid., B, III, 13.

BUT, Sir, the mind must be employed, and we grow weary when idle.

That is, Sir, because, others being busy, we want company; but if we were all idle, there would be no growing weary; we should all entertain one another.

Ibid., II, 98.

I HAVE risen every morning since New year's day, at about eight; when I was up, I have indeed done but little; yet it is no slight advancement to obtain for so many hours more, the consciousness of being.

Ibid., 17.

DISORDER I have found one great cause of idleness.
Dr. Johnson, B, I, 436.

To be idle and to be poor have always been reproaches,
and therefore every man endeavours with his utmost
care to hide his poverty from others, and his idleness
from himself. *Ibid., Idler,* No. 17.

I LOOK upon indolence as a sort of suicide; for the
man is effectually destroyed, though the appetites of
the brute may survive.

Chesterfield, 609.

EXPECT poison from the standing water.

Blake.

PASTIME, like wine, is poison in the morning.
Thomas Fuller, H, 174.

No one will set heartily to work, who has the face
to enter a strange house, ask the master of it for
a considerable loan . . . and walk off with it in his
pocket. You might as well suspect a highwayman
of addicting himself to hard study in the intervals of
his profession.

Hazlitt, L R, II, 259.

EVERYTHING that doth us good is so apt to do us hurt
too, that it is a strong Argument for Men to be quiet.
Halifax, 254.

IF Men would think more, they would act less.

Ibid.

AN inability to stay quiet, an irritable desire to act
directly, is one of the most conspicuous failings of
mankind. *Bagehot, P,* 186.

CONTENT layeth Pleasure, nay Virtue, in a Slumber, with few and faint Intermissions.

It is to the Mind, like Moss to a Tree, it bindeth it up so as to stop its Growth.

Halifax, 248.

A MAN that will enjoy a quiet conscience must lead a quiet life.

Chesterfield, 761.

SOME register the changes of the wind, and die fully convinced that the wind is changeable.

Dr. Johnson, Idler, No. 17.

ACT if you like—but you do it at your peril. Men's actions are too strong for them. Show me a man who has acted, and who has not been the victim and slave of his action.

Emerson, E, I, 500.

THE person that has acted, fears; the person that looks on is formidable.

Ibid., J, V, 42.

OUR dignity is not in what we do, but what we understand. The whole world is doing things.

Santayana, E, 202.

XXV

SOLITUDE

SOLITUDE is dangerous to reason, without being favourable to virtue.

Dr. Johnson, M, I, 219.

REMEMBER that the solitary mortal is certainly luxurious, probably superstitious, and possibly mad.

Ibid.

THERE are some solitary wretches, who seem to have left the rest of mankind only as Eve left Adam, to meet the devil in private.

Pope, 293.

SOLITUDE is impracticable, and society fatal.

Emerson, E, III, 10.

THE young spirit pants to enter society. But all the ways of culture and greatness lead to solitary imprisonment.

Ibid., I, 453.

IT is very seldom that a man is truly alone. He needs to retire as much from his solitude as he does from society. . . . There is one means of procuring solitude which to me, and I apprehend to all men, is effectual, and that is to go to the window and look at the stars.

Ibid., J, III, 263.

SOCIETY is like the air, necessary to breathe, but insufficient to live on.

Santayana, V.

A LITTLE society is needful to show a man his failings.

R. L. Stevenson, E, 82.

You could read Kant by yourself, if you wanted; but you must share a joke with some one else.

R. L. Stevenson, V, 17.

COMPANY is an extreme Provocative to Fancy; and like a hot Bed in Gardening, is apt to make our Imaginations sprout too fast.

Shaftesbury, I, 159.

BUT little do Men perceive what Solitude is, and how far it extendeth. For a Crowd is not Company; and Faces are but a Gallery of Pictures; and Talk but a tinkling Cymbal, where there is no Love.

Bacon, E, 92.

IN solitude we have our dreams to ourselves, and in company we agree to dream in concert.

Dr. Johnson, Idler, No. 32.

MEN that cannot entertain themselves want somebody, though they care for nobody.

Halifax, 242.

XXVI

FRIENDSHIP

FRIENDSHIP is to be purchased only by friendship.   A man may have authority over others; but he can never have their heart but by giving his own.

Bishop Wilson, M, 52.

A MAN is to go about his own Business as if he had not a Friend in the World to help him in it.

Halifax, 245.

IT is a Misfortune for a Man not to have a Friend in the World, but for that reason he shall have no Enemy.

Ibid., 243.

IT is some kind of Scandal not to bear with the Faults of an honest Man.

Ibid., 245.

IF you want a person's faults, go to those who love him. They will not tell you, but they know.

R. L. Stevenson, B, 159.

THOSE Friends who are above Interest are seldom above Jealousy.

Halifax, 243.

FRIENDSHIP cannot live with Ceremony, nor without Civility.

Ibid.

MAKE not a Bosom Friend of a melancholy sad Soul: . . . he goes always heavy loaded, and thou must bear half.

Dr. Fuller, I, 102.

BEWARE, I say, beware, how thou fallest in with indigent Friends. I never took such uneasy Steps in my Life as I have done when I was fettered and clogged with such. Their endless Necessities and Sorrows gave me everlasting Unhappiness. They never let me possess my own Money that I had provided for my Occasions and Designs, but constantly wrung it out of me, and kept me almost as Necessitous as themselves. . . . But that which gave me the greatest Vexation of all was, I could never do any of them any good. I have had several such, and give thee this Warning to avoid the like, as thou wouldest an evil spirit.

Dr. Fuller, I, 215.

I ADVISE thee to visit thy Relations and friends; but I advise thee not to live too near them.

Ibid., 33.

To make a Man tell of some private Grievance, pretend the like Uneasiness, and seem sick of the same Disease.

Ibid., 200.

MOST people enjoy the inferiority of their best friends.
Chesterfield, 353.

WHOEVER contracts a friendship with a knave or a fool, has something bad to do or to conceal.

Ibid., 633.

FRIENDSHIP between mortals can be contracted on no other terms than that one must some time mourn for the other's death.

Dr. Johnson, R, No. 17.

THE most fatal disease of friendship is gradual decay, or dislike hourly increased by causes too slender for complaint, and too numerous for removal.

Dr. Johnson, Idler, No. 23.

KINDNESS . . is in our power, but fondness is not.

Ibid., B, IV, 154.

FRIENDSHIP, like love, is destroyed by long absence, though it may be increased by short intermissions.

Ibid., Idler, No. 23.

IF a man does not make new acquaintance as he advances through life, he will soon find himself left alone. A man, Sir, should keep his friendship in constant repair.

Ibid., B, I, 300.

SIR, I look upon every day to be lost, in which I do not make a new acquaintance.

Ibid., IV, 374.

IN youth we are apt to be too rigorous in our expectations, and to suppose that the duties of life are to be performed with unfailing exactness and regularity; but in our progress through life we are forced to abate much of our demands, and to take friends such as we can find them, not as we would make them.

These concessions every wise man is more ready to make to others, as he knows that he shall often want them for himself; and when he remembers how often he fails in the observance or cultivation of his best friends, is willing to suppose that his friends may in their turn neglect him, without any intention to offend him.

Ibid., L, I, 100.

ALWAYS, Sir, set a high value on spontaneous kindness. He whose inclination prompts him to cultivate your friendship of his own accord, will love you more than one whom you have been at pains to attach to you.
Dr. Johnson, B, IV, 115.

NOTHING is more common than mutual dislike, where mutual approbation is particularly expected.
Ibid., III, 423.

NEXT to him who is compelled to trust, I think him unhappy who is chosen to be trusted. *Ibid., R,* No. 13.

THE vanity of being known to be trusted with a secret is generally one of the chief motives to disclose it.
Ibid.

A MAN has no excuse for betraying the secrets of his friends, unless he also divulges his own.
Hazlitt, C, 53.

SHY and unready men are great betrayers of secrets; for there are few wants more urgent for the moment than the want of something to say.
Sir Henry Taylor, S, 131.

THE discussing the characters and foibles of common friends is a great sweetener and cement of friendship.
Hazlitt, T T, II, 78.

I LIKE a friend the better for having faults that one can talk about. *Ibid., P S,* I, 318.

WE grow tired of everything but turning others into ridicule, and congratulating ourselves on their defects.
Ibid., 320.

OLD friends are best. King James used to call for his old shoes; they were easiest for his feet.

Selden, 49.

OLD friendships are like meats served up repeatedly, cold, comfortless, and distasteful. The stomach turns against them.

Hazlitt, P S, I, 315.

SHY and proud men . . . are more liable than any others to fall into the hands of parasites and creatures of low character. For in the intimacies which are formed by shy men, they do not choose, but are chosen.

Sir Henry Taylor, S, 27.

IN prosperity our friends know us; in adversity we know our friends.

Churton Collins, E, 95.

THE spice of life is battle; the friendliest relations are still a kind of contest, . . . and every durable bond between human beings is founded in or heightened by some element of competition.

R. L. Stevenson, M, 146.

OUR chief want in life is, somebody who shall make us do what we can.

Emerson, E, II, 337.

BETWEEN cultivated minds the first interview is the best.

Ibid., J, III, 496.

FRIENDS are fictions founded on some single momentary experience.

Ibid., X, 11.

MEN cease to interest us when we find their limitations.
Emerson, E, I, 165.

A MAN's growth is seen in the successive choirs of his friends.

Ibid., 164.

WHY insist on rash personal relations with your friend? . . . Let him be to thee for ever a sort of beautiful enemy.

Ibid., 114.

DEAR heart, take it sadly home to thee, that there will and can be no co-operation.

Ibid., J, VII, 140.

IN the last analysis, love is only the reflection of a man's own worthiness from other men.

Ibid., E, I, 116.

XXVII

SYMPATHY, BENEVOLENCE

ALL are apt to shrink from those that lean upon them.
Halifax, 246.

WHEN we describe our sensations of another's sorrows,
either in friendly or ceremonious condolence, the cus-
toms of the world scarcely admit of rigid veracity.
Dr. Johnson, Idler, No. 50.

SIR, that sympathetic feeling goes a very little way in
depressing the mind.
Ibid., B, II, 94.

THE least pain in our little finger gives us more concern and uneasiness, than the destruction of millions
of our fellow-beings.
Hazlitt, W, X, 324.

THOSE who do not feel pain seldom think that it is felt.
Dr. Johnson, R, No. 48.

PEOPLE in distress never think that you feel enough.
Ibid., B, II, 469.

MEN that talk of their own benefits, are not believed
to talk of them because they have done them, but to
have done them because they might talk of them.
Ben Jonson, 403.

EVERY one in this world has as much as they can do in
caring for themselves, and few have leisure really to
think of their neighbour's distresses, however they may
delight their tongues with talking of them.
Dr. Johnson, M, I, 268.

A SYMPATHETIC person is placed in the dilemma of a swimmer among drowning men, who all catch at him, and if he give so much as a leg or a finger, they will drown him.

Emerson, E, I, 243.

THERE is a hook in every benefit, that sticks in his jaws that takes that benefit, and draws him whither the Benefactor will.

Donne, 550.

LEARN how to refuse favours. This is a great and very useful Art.

Dr Fuller, I, 19.

XXVIII

GRATITUDE

I am of an Opinion, in which I am every Day more confirmed by Observation, that Gratitude is one of those things that cannot be bought. It must be born with Men, or else all the Obligations in the World will not create it. An outward Show may be made to satisfy Decency, and to prevent Reproach; but a real Sense of a kind thing is a Gift of Nature, and never was, nor can be acquired.

Halifax, 205.

GRATITUDE is a burden upon our imperfect nature.
Chesterfield, 628.

THE great effect of friendship is beneficence, yet by the first act of uncommon kindness it is endangered, like plants that bear their fruit and die.

Dr. Johnson, R, No. 64.

THERE are minds so impatient of inferiority, that their gratitude is a species of revenge, and they return benefits, not because recompense is a pleasure, but because obligation is a pain.

Ibid., No. 87.

To quicken the Memory of past Kindness thou hast done to any one, is a very nice Point to manage.

Dr. Fuller, II, 131.

To accept a favour from a friend is to confer one.
Churton Collins, E, 98.

WE do not quite forgive a giver. The hand that feeds us is in some danger of being bitten.

Emerson, E, I, 286.

XXIX

ADVICE

CERTAINLY, to give Advice to a Friend, either asked or unasked, is so far from a Fault, that it is a Duty; but if a Man love to give Advice, it is a sure sign that he himself wanteth it.

Halifax, 244.

A MAN whilst he is advising putteth his Understanding upon Tiptoes, and is unwilling to bring it down again.

Ibid.

WHEN Men are easy in themselves, they let others remain so.

Shaftesbury, III, 109.

THEY have a Right to censure, that have a Heart to help.

Wm. Penn, 15.

MANY a friend will tell us our faults without reserve, who will not so much as hint at our follies.

Chesterfield, 123.

IF a friend tell thee a fault, imagine always that he telleth thee not the whole.

Dr. Fuller, I, 47.

ADVICE is offensive, not because it . . . convicts us of any fault which had escaped our notice, but because it shows us that we are known to others as well as to ourselves.

Dr. Johnson, R, 155.

To profit from good advice requires more wisdom than to give it.

Churton Collins, E, 100.

XXX

LOVE

WE must not ridicule a passion which he who never felt never was happy, and he who laughs at never deserves to feel—a passion which has caused the change of empires, and the loss of worlds—a passion which has inspired heroism and subdued avarice.

Dr. Johnson, M, I, 290.

MEN have died from time to time, and worms have eaten them, but not for love.

As You Like It, IV, 1.

AFFECTION should not be too sharp-eyed, and love is not to be made by magnifying glasses.

Sir Thomas Browne, C, 70.

ANOTHER misery there is in affection, that whom we truly love like our own, we forget their looks, nor can our memory retain the Idea of their faces.

Ibid., R, 145.

THAT which is to be loved long must be loved with reason rather than with passion.

Dr. Johnson, Idler, No. 59.

FEW (especially young) people know how to love, or how to hate; their love is an unbounded weakness, fatal to the person they love; their hate is a hot, rash, and imprudent violence, always fatal to themselves.

Chesterfield, 557.

LOVE is a talkative passion.

Bishop Wilson, S, 194.

Passion plucks no berries from the myrtle and ivy. . . .
Where there is leisure for fiction there is little grief.
Dr. Johnson, W, II, 148.

There are charms made only for distant admiration.
No spectacle is nobler than a blaze.

Ibid., 228.

Love is uniform, but courtship is perpetually varying:
the different arts of gallantry, which beauty has inspired, would of themselves be sufficient to fill a volume.
Ibid., A, No. 95.

Were it not for imagination, Sir, a man would be as
happy in the arms of a chambermaid as of a Duchess.
Ibid., B, III, 341.

If things were seen as they truly are, the beauty of
bodies would be much abridged.
Sir Thomas Browne, C, 70.

Absences are a good influence in love and keep it
bright and delicate.
R. L. Stevenson, V, 21.

Love is only one of many passions . . . and it has no
great influence on the sum of life.
Dr. Johnson, W, IX, 244.

It is as safe to play with Fire, as it is to dally with
Gallantry. Love is a passion that hath Friends in the
Garrison.

Halifax, 31.

One unguarded look betrayed David.
Bishop Wilson, S, 151.

MEN and women call one another inconstant, and accuse one another of having changed their minds, when, God knows, they have but changed the object of their eye, and seen a better white or red.

Donne, 483.

EVEN an inconstant flame may burn brightly, if the soul is naturally combustible.

Santayana, R, II, 25.

MAKE love to the most impertinent beauty of condition that you meet with, and be gallant with all the rest.

Chesterfield, 291.

THERE are few things that we so unwillingly give up, even in an advanced age, as the supposition that we have still the power of ingratiating ourselves with the fair sex.

Dr. Johnson, M, II, 326.

IF anyone complains in not succeeding in affairs of gallantry, we will venture to say, it is because he is not gallant.   He has mistaken his talent.

Hazlitt, R T, I, 116.

OF the uses of adversity which are sweet, none are sweeter than those which grow out of disappointed love.

Sir Henry Taylor, N, 78.

MEN who do not make advances to women are apt to become victims to women who make advances to them.

Bagehot, B, 314.

THE man's desire is for the woman; but the woman's desire is rarely other than for the desire of the man.

Coleridge, T T, 75.

IN women pity begets love, in men love begets pity.
Churton Collins, E, 99.

ALL mankind love a lover.
Emerson, E, I, 93.

NOT always can flowers, pearls, poetry, protestations, nor even home in another heart, content the awful soul that dwells in clay.

Ibid., 100.

ALL the veneration of Spring connects itself with love. . . . Even the frog and his mate have a new and gayer coat for this benign occasion.

Ibid., J, IX, 178.

YOUNG men make great mistakes in life; for one thing, they idealize love too much.

Jowett, 252.

XXXI

MARRIAGE

THERE is, indeed, nothing that so much seduces reason from vigilance, as the thought of passing life with an amiable woman; and if all would happen that a lover fancies, I know not what other terrestrial happiness would deserve pursuit.

Dr. Johnson, B, I, 381.

MARRIAGE is a desperate thing. The frogs in Æsop were extreme wise; they had a great mind to some water, but they would not leap into the well, because they could not get out again.

Selden, 75.

OF all actions of a man's life, his marriage does least concern other people; yet of all actions of our life, 'tis most meddled with by other people.

Ibid.

'TIS reason, a man that will have a wife should be at the charge of all her Trinkets, and pay all the scores she sets him on. He that will keep a Monkey, 'tis fit he should pay for the glasses she breaks.

Ibid., 139.

WIVES are young Men's Mistresses; Companions for middle Age; and old Men's Nurses.

Bacon, E, 24.

THE Muscovite women esteem none loving husbands except they beat their wives.

Thomas Fuller, H, 175.

BETTER to sit up all night, than to go to bed with a Dragon.　*Jeremy Taylor, H*, 213.

NEXT to the danger of committing the Fault yourself, the greatest is that of seeing it in your Husband.

Halifax, 10.

A WIFE is to thank God her Husband hath faults. . . . A Husband without Faults is a dangerous Observer.

Ibid., 12.

BE not hasty to marry; it's better to have one Plough going than two Cradles; and more Profit to have a Barn filled, than a Bed.

Dr. Fuller, II, 40.

IF thou marriest a rich Wife, thou art sure to have somewhat to be in Love withal.

Ibid., 13.

KEEP thy Eyes wide open before Marriage; and half shut afterwards. *Ibid.*, 4.

FIRST get an absolute conquest over thyself, and then thou wilt easily govern thy Wife.

Ibid., I, 26.

THE reason why so few marriages are happy, is because young ladies spend their time in making nets, not in making cages.

Swift, III, 400.

IN matters of religion and matrimony I never give any advice; because I will not have anybody's torments in this world or the next laid to my charge.

Chesterfield, 1327.

TO take a wife merely as an agreeable and rational companion, will commonly be found to be a grand mistake. *Ibid.*, 1328.

THERE are but two objects in marriage, love or money. If you marry for love, you will certainly have some very happy days, and probably many very uneasy ones; if for money, you will have no happy days and probably no uneasy ones. *Chesterfield*, 654.

IT is possible, though not very probable, that there may be joy in marriage. *Ibid.*, 1021.

WHEN a wife or mistress lives as in a jail, the person that confines her lives the life of a jailor.

Shenstone, 279.

IT is commonly a weak man who marries for love.
Dr. Johnson, B, III, 3.

THEN, Sir, you are not of opinion with some who imagine that certain men and certain women are made for each other; and that they cannot be happy if they miss their counterparts.

To be sure not, Sir. I believe marriages would in general be as happy, and often more so, if they were all made by the Lord Chancellor.

Ibid., II, 461.

SIR, it is so far from being natural for a man and woman to live in a state of marriage, that we find all the motives which they have for remaining in that connection, and the restraints which civilized society imposes to prevent separation, are hardly sufficient to keep them together.

Ibid., 165.

SOME cunning men choose fools for their wives, think-ing to manage them, but they always fail.

Ibid., V, 226.

A SMALL country town is not the place in which one would choose to quarrel with a wife; every human being in such places is a spy.

Dr. Johnson, L, I, 107.

No man likes to live under the eye of perpetual disapprobation.

Ibid., B, III, 181.

No man will be fond of what forces him daily to feel himself inferior.

Ibid., M, I, 256.

A MAN is in general better pleased when he has a good dinner upon his table, than when his wife talks Greek.

Ibid., II, 11.

A MAN will sometimes rage at his wife, when in reality his mistress has offended him; and a lady complain of the cruelty of her husband, when she has no other enemy than bad cards.

Ibid., R, No. 18.

MARRIAGE has many pains, but celibacy has no pleasures

Ibid., W, XI, 74.

THEY that have grown old in a single state are generally found to be morose, fretful, and captious.

Ibid., R, No. 112.

THEY act as beings under the constant sense of some known inferiority, that fills their minds with rancour, and their tongues with censure.

Ibid., W, XI, 73.

MARRIAGE is not commonly unhappy, otherwise than as life is unhappy.

Dr. Johnson, R, No. 45.

NOTWITHSTANDING all that wit, or malice, or pride, or prudence will be able to suggest, men and women must at last pass their lives together.

Ibid., No. 119.

I BELIEVE it will be found that those who marry late are best pleased with their children, and those who marry early with their partners.

Ibid., W, XI, 83.

MR. JOHNSON, would you advise me to marry?

I would advise no man to marry, Sir, who is not likely to propagate understanding.

Ibid., M, I, 213.

YOU may observe that I am well-bred to a degree of needless scrupulosity.

Ibid., 169.

MARRIAGE has, as you say, no *natural* relation to love. Marriage belongs to society; it is a social contract.

Coleridge, T T, 450.

THERE can be only one end to marriage without love, and that is love without marriage.

Churton Collins, E, 96.

DOMESTIC flattery is the most dangerous of all flatteries.

Sir Henry Taylor, S, 69.

IF they only married when they fell in love, most people would die unwed.

R. L. Stevenson, V, 10.

MARRIAGE

MARRIAGE is a step so grave and decisive that it attracts light-headed variable men by its very awfulness.

R. L. Stevenson, V, 23.

MARRIAGE is one long conversation, chequered by disputes.

Ibid., M, 189.

THE best of men and the best of women may sometimes live together all their lives, and .   hold each other lost spirits to the end.

Ibid., V, 16.

ONCE you are married, there is nothing left for you, not even suicide, but to be good.

Ibid., 34.

XXXII

WOMEN

As the faculty of writing has been chiefly a masculine endowment, the reproach of making the world miserable has been always thrown upon the women.

Dr. Johnson, R, No. 18.

A WOMAN, the more curious she is about her face, is commonly the more careless about her house.

Ben Jonson, 392.

No woman ever hates a man for being in love with her; but many a woman hates a man for being a friend to her.

Pope, 305.

NATURE has given women so much power that the law has very wisely given them little.

Dr. Johnson, L, I, 104.

A WOMAN's preaching is like a dog's walking on his hinder legs. It is not done well; but you are surprised to find it done at all.

Ibid., B, I, 463.

WOMEN commonly eat more sparingly, and are less curious in the choice of meat; but if once you find a woman gluttonous, expect from her very little virtue.

Ibid., L, II, 323.

WOMEN have a perpetual envy of our vices; they are less vicious than we, not from choice, but because we restrict them.

Ibid., B, IV, 291.

WOMAN's beauty, like men's wit, is generally fatal to the owners, unless directed by a judgment which seldom accompanies a great degree of either.

Chesterfield, W, II, 101.

LADIES grow handsome by looking at themselves in the glass.

Hazlitt, P S, II, 52.

WOMEN are not formed for great cares themselves, but to soothe and soften ours.

Chesterfield, W, II, 95.

As we descend into the vale of years our infirmities require some domestic female society.

Gibbon, M, I, 202.

BY permitting your reflection to carry you from your society, you expose yourself to very hazardous conjectures.

Countess Dowager of Carlisle, 94.

SPELL well, if you can.

Ibid., 116.

ALMOST every woman described to you by a woman present a tragic idea, and not an idea of well-being.

Emerson, J, V, 25.

A WOMAN who is confuted is never convinced.

Churton Collins, E, 99.

WOMEN are always on the defensive.

Ibid., 98.

WHAT attracts us in a woman rarely binds us to her.

Ibid., 101.

XXXIII

THE FAMILY

THE family is one of nature's masterpieces.

Santayana, R, II, 35.

THE building up of a Family is a Manufacture very little above the building a House of Cards.

Halifax, 250.

A FAMILY is but too often a commonwealth of malignants.

Pope, 299.

HE that loves not his wife and children, feeds a Lioness at home, and broods a nest of sorrow.

Jeremy Taylor, S, I, 236.

IT takes patience to appreciate domestic bliss; volatile spirits prefer unhappiness.

Santayana, R, II, 45.

IN every house there is a good deal of false hospitality. Relatives come thither of all the degrees of cousindom and family acquaintances, who, like cats, frequent the place and not the man

Emerson, J, V, 270.

MOST of the persons whom I see in my own house I see across a gulf.

Ibid., 324.

IS not a small house best? Put a woman into a small house, and after five years she comes out large and healthy.

Ibid., VII, 47.

CHILDREN sweeten labours; but they make Misfortunes more bitter: they increase the Cares of Life; but they mitigate the Remembrance of Death.

Bacon, E, 21.

WE think our Children a Part of ourselves, though as they grow up they might very well undeceive us.

Halifax, 250.

LOVE is presently out of Breath when it is to go up Hill, from the Children to the Parents.

Ibid.

YOU are to have as strict a Guard upon yourself amongst your Children, as if you were amongst your Enemies.

Ibid., 23.

As fathers commonly go, it is seldom a misfortune to be fatherless; and considering the general run of sons, as seldom a misfortune to be childless.

Chesterfield, 471.

FEW fathers care much for their sons, or at least, most of them care more for their money. . . . Of those who really love their sons, few know how to do it.

Ibid., 521.

THE regal and parental tyrant differ only in the extent of their dominions, and the number of their slaves.

Dr. Johnson, R, No. 148.

THERE must always be a struggle between a father and a son, while one aims at power and the other at independence.

Ibid., B, I, 427.

CHILDREN and subjects . . . are much seldomer in the wrong than parents and Kings.

Chesterfield, 1075.

HOME is the girl's prison and the woman's workhouse.

Bernard Shaw, 240.

SOME admiring what motives to mirth infants meet with in their silent and solitary smiles, have resolved (how truly I know not) that then they converse with angels.

Thomas Fuller, P, IV.

ONE cannot love lumps of flesh, and little infants are nothing more.

Dr. Johnson, M, I, 328.

BABIES do not want to hear about babies; they like to be told of giants and castles, and of somewhat which can stretch and stimulate their little minds.

Ibid., 156.

You teach your daughters the diameters of the planets, and wonder when you have done that they do not delight in your company. *Ibid.*, 160.

NOTHING seems to have been more universally dreaded by the ancients than orbity, or want of children.

Ibid., R, No. 69.

FEW parents act in such a manner as much to enforce their maxims by the credit of their lives.

Ibid., W, XI, 72.

IF you strike a child, take care that you strike it in anger, even at the risk of maiming it for life. A blow in cold blood neither can nor should be forgiven.

Bernard Shaw, 234

A SPOILT child never loves its mother.

> *Sir Henry Taylor, N, 123.*

FATHERS wish to be fathers of the mind as well as of the body of their children. But in my experience they seem to be merely the occasion of new beings coming into the world.

> *Emerson, J, IV, 80*

BAD to see a row of children looking old.

> *Ibid., 402.*

CHILDREN are all foreigners. We treat them as such.

> *Ibid., V, 261.*

XXXIV

THE WORLD

THE world is a country which nobody ever yet knew by description; one must travel through it one's self to be acquainted with it.

Chesterfield, 60.

THE World is a great Cheat.

Dr. Fuller, I, 51.

A MAN that steps aside from the World, and hath leisure to observe it without Interest or Design, thinks all Mankind as mad as they think him.

Halifax, 231.

SINGULARITY may be good Sense at home, but it must not go much abroad.

Ibid., 254.

THE greatest Part of the Business of the World, is the Effect of not thinking.

Ibid.

SYLLABLES govern the world. *Selden*, 100.

HE was a wise Pope, that when one that was used to be merry with him, before he was advanced to the Popedom, refrained afterwards to come at him, presuming he was busy in governing the Christian world. The Pope sends for him, bids him come again; and, says he, we will be merry as we were before, for thou little thinkest what a little foolery governs the whole world. *Ibid.*, 97.

To understand the World, and to like it, are two things not easily to be reconciled.

Halifax, 230.

THE World is nothing but Vanity cut out into several Shapes.

Halifax, 240.

THE meaning of the word vanity never crosses the vulgar heart.

Santayana, E, 82.

THE world, in its best state, is nothing more than a larger assembly of beings, combining to counterfeit happiness which they do not feel.

Dr. Johnson, A, No. 120.

To know the world is necessary, . . . and to know it early is convenient, if it be only that we may learn early to despise it.

Ibid., Idler, No. 80.

IT is one of the most difficult things in life, to know when one has enough of the world.

Bishop Wilson, M, 132.

THE world would use us just as it did the martyrs, if we loved God as they did.

Ibid., 90.

THE world will, in the end, follow only those who have despised as well as served it.

Samuel Butler, N, 365.

THE world, like an accomplished hostess, pays most attention to those whom it will soonest forget.

Churton Collins, E, 95.

THE world will commonly end by making men that which it thinks them.

Sir Henry Taylor, S, 135.

HAPPY the man who, with a certain fund of parts and knowledge, gets acquainted with the world early enough to make it his bubble, at an age when most people are the bubbles of the world! *Chesterfield*, 436.

I AM at this time acquainted with many elderly people, who have all passed their whole lives in the great world, but with such levity and inattention that they know no more of it now than they did at fifteen.

Ibid., 38.

NOTHING is in general more gloomy and monotonous than declamations on the hollowness and transitoriness of human life and grandeur.

Matthew Arnold, 434.

THE mind must have some worldly objects to excite its attention, otherwise it will stagnate in indolence, sink into melancholy, or rise into visions and enthusiasm.

Chesterfield, 1050.

WHEN I reflect back upon what I have seen, what I have heard, and what I have done myself, I can hardly persuade myself that all that frivolous hurry and bustle, and pleasures of the world, had any reality; but they seem to have been the dreams of restless nights.

Ibid., 1262.

SHAKESPEARE'S fault that the world appears so empty. He has educated you with his painted world, and this real one seems a huckster's shop.

Emerson, *J*, VII, 140.

IT is the Fools and Knaves that make the Wheels of the World turn. *They* are *the World*; those few who have Sense or Honesty sneak up and down single, but never go in Herds. *Halifax*, 231.

XXXV

FOOLS AND FOLLY

A FOOL hath no Dialogue within himself, the first Thought carrieth him without the Reply of a second.

Halifax, 236.

A FOOL's Paradise is a wise man's hell.

Thomas Fuller, H, 320

SOME Men's Heads are as easily blown away as their Hats.

Halifax, 241.

A BUSY Fool is fitter to be shut up than a downright Madman.

Ibid., 235.

LISTEN to the fool's reproach! It is a kingly title!

Blake.

To make a trade of laughing at a fool is the highway to become one.

Thomas Fuller, H, 172.

ONE should no more laugh at a contemptible Fool than at a dead Fly.

Halifax, 235.

IT is hard to find a Blockhead so wise as to be upon the Defensive; he will be sallying, and then he is sure to be ill-used.

Ibid., 235.

A BLOCKHEAD is as ridiculous when he talketh, as is a Goose when it flieth.

Ibid.

THE Vanity of teaching often tempteth a Man to forget he is a Blockhead.

Ibid., 240.

As Rivers which run very slowly have always the most Mud at the bottom, so a solid stiffness in the constant course of a man's Life is a sign of a thick bed of Mud at the bottom of his Brain.

Halifax, 149.

IN the world a man will often be reputed to be a man of sense, only because he is not a man of talent.

Sir Henry Taylor, S, 29.

NATURE delights in punishing stupid people.

Emerson, J, V, 238.

FOLLY is often more cruel in the Consequence, than Malice can be in the Intent.

Halifax, 235.

TILL Follies become ruinous, the World is better with than it would be without them.

Ibid., 236.

THE most ingenious way of becoming foolish, is by a System.   *Shaftesbury*, I, 290.

THE liker anything is to Wisdom, if it be not plainly the thing itself, the more directly it becomes its opposite.   *Ibid.*

CARDINAL DE RETZ very sagaciously marked out Cardinal Chigi for a little mind, from the moment that he told him he had wrote three years with the same pen, and that it was an excellent good one still.

Chesterfield, 231.

I ALWAYS treat fools and coxcombs with great ceremony; true good breeding not being a sufficient barrier against them.   *Ibid.*, 506.

152

ALMOST all absurdity of conduct arises from the imitation of those whom we cannot resemble.

Dr. Johnson, R, No. 135.

SOLOMON laid hold of folly, as well as wisdom, that he might see what was good for the Sons of Men.

Dr. Fuller, I, 188.

THE word Folly is, perhaps, the prettiest word in the language.   *Shenstone,* 208.

IF the fool would persist in his folly he would become wise.   *Blake.*

IF others had not been foolish, we should be so

Ibid.

FOLLY is as often owing to a want of proper sentiments as to a want of understanding.

Hazlitt, Sh, 9.

THE greatest hypocrites are the greatest dupes.

Ibid., C, 43.

A FOOL or idiot is one who expects things to happen that never can happen.

George Eliot, Felix Holt.

THE most positive men are the most credulous.

Pope, 297.

I AM always afraid of a fool.   One cannot be sure that he is not a knave as well.

Hazlitt, C, 85.

A WAY foolishness has of revenging itself is to excommunicate the world.

Santayana, E, 112.

XXXVI

KNAVES

THE Mixture of Fool and Knave maketh up the parti-
coloured Creatures that make all the Bustle in the
World.

Halifax, 233.

THE Eagerness of a Knave maketh him often as catch-
able as Ignorance maketh a Fool.

Ibid., 232.

IF Knaves had not foolish Memories, they would
never trust one another so often as they do.

Ibid., 233.

MEN given to dissembling are like Rooks at play, they
will cheat for Shillings, they are so used to it.

Ibid., 192.

WEAK Men are apt to be cruel, because they stick at
nothing that may repair the ill Effect of their Mistakes.

Ibid., 235.

MANY Men *swallow* the being cheated, but no Man
could ever endure to chew it.

Ibid., 247.

THERE are more Fools than Knaves in the world, else
the Knaves would not have enough to live upon.

Samuel Butler, author of Hudibras, 474.

GRAVITY is of the very Essence of Imposture.

Shaftesbury, I, 11.

EVERY man wishes to be wise, and they who cannot be
wise are almost always cunning.

Dr. Johnson, Idler, No. 92.

IT should seem that indolence itself would incline a person to be honest; as it requires infinitely greater pains and contrivance to be a knave.

Shenstone, 228.

CUNNING is the dark sanctuary of incapacity.

Chesterfield, 656.

ALWAYS be ready to speak your mind, and a base man will avoid you.

Blake.

THE fox condemns the trap, not himself.

Ibid.

THE weakest man in the world can avail himself of the passion of the wisest.

Chesterfield, 572.

SOME persons make promises for the pleasure of breaking them.

Hazlitt, C, 145.

CLEVER men are the tools with which bad men work.

Ibid., W, XI, 340.

WE love force and we care very little how it is exhibited.

Emerson, J, V, 262.

XXXVII

PRUDENCE

THE most necessary thing in the World, and yet the least usual, is to reflect that those we deal with may know how to be as arrant Knaves as ourselves.

Halifax, 232.

MEN must be saved in this World by their Want of Faith.

Ibid., 245.

THE best Qualification of a Prophet is to have a good Memory.

Ibid., 249.

SUSPICION is rather a Virtue than a fault, as long as it doth like a Dog that *watcheth*, and doth *not bite*.

Ibid., 247

WHEN our Suspicion of another Man is once dis-covered by him, there ought to be an end of all further Commerce.

Ibid.

A WISE Man, in trusting another, must not rely upon his *Promise* against his *Nature*.

Ibid.

THE best way to suppose what may come, is to remem-ber what is past.

Ibid., 249.

TAKE care how thou offendest Men raised from low condition.

Dr. Fuller, I, 83.

AVOID the company of those that are very Poor and Necessitous.

Dr. Fuller, I, 79.

THOUGH thou art not to let the Sun set on thy Anger, yet thou art not to trust a deceiving treacherous Enemy next Morning.

Ibid., 55.

LET not thy Will roar, when thy Power can but whisper.

Ibid., 14.

IF thou hast a Suit to any one, . . . come up on him unexpectedly, and push it home at once.

Ibid., II, 131.

DISTRUST all those who love you extremely upon a very slight acquaintance, and without any visible reason. Be upon your guard, too, against those who confess as their weaknesses all the cardinal virtues.

Chesterfield, 573.

WHEN you have found out the prevailing passion of any man, remember never to trust him where that passion is concerned.

Ibid., 38.

SUSPECT, in general, those who remarkably affect any one virtue. . . . I say suspect them, for they are commonly impostors; but do not be sure that they are always so; for I have sometimes known saints really religious, blusterers really brave, reformers of manners really honest, and prudes really chaste.

Ibid., 296.

NEVER trust a man who speaks well of everybody.
Churton Collins, E, 101.

ALWAYS mistrust a subordinate who never finds fault
with his superior.

Ibid., 98.

PLAUSIBILITIES and pretensions are the most direct
index to the defects of men.

Sir Henry Taylor, S, 20.

IN our judgment of men, we are to beware of giving
any great importance to occasional acts. By acts of
occasional virtue weak men endeavour to redeem
themselves in their own estimation, vain men to exalt
themselves in that of mankind.

Ibid.

IT is only shallow people who do not judge by appearances.

Oscar Wilde, 63.

PEOPLE unused to the world have babbling countenances; and are unskilful enough to show what they
have sense enough not to tell.

Chesterfield, 515.

IT almost violates the proprieties, if we say above the
breath here what the confessing eyes do not hesitate
to utter to every street passenger.

Emerson, E, II, 284.

THERE is an unseemly exposure of the mind, as well
as of the body.

Hazlitt, S E, 165.

There are some occasions in which a man must tell half his secret, in order to conceal the rest; but there is seldom one in which a man should tell it all.

Chesterfield, 575.

A secret may be sometimes best kept by keeping the secret of its being a secret.

Sir Henry Taylor, S, 128.

It is very disagreeable to seem reserved, and very dangerous not to be so.

Chesterfield, 62.

It is dangerous to be sincere unless you are also stupid.

Bernard Shaw, 243.

Men of the world, knowing that there are few things so unpopular as penetration, take care to wear the appearance of being imposed upon.

Sir Henry Taylor, S, 21.

He who has suffered you to impose on him, knows you.

Blake.

A wise man, like the moon, only shows his bright side to the world.

Churton Collins, E, 96.

There is often less danger in the things we fear than in the things we desire.

Ibid., 100.

Prudence keeps life safe, but does not often make it happy.

Dr. Johnson, Idler, No. 57.

XXXVIII

SUCCESS AND FAILURE

A FOOL often fails because he thinks what is difficult is easy, and a wise man because he thinks what is easy is difficult.

Churton Collins, E, 100.

A DIFFICULTY raiseth the Spirits of a great Man, he hath a mind to wrestle with it, and give it a Fall.

A Man's Mind must be very low, if the Difficulty doth not make a part of his Pleasure.

The Pride of Compassing may more than compare with the Pleasure of Enjoying.

Halifax, 248.

THOSE who are disposed to be wise too late, are apt to be valiant too early.

Ibid., 227.

HE that leaveth nothing to Chance will do few things ill, but he will do very few things.

Ibid., 247.

WISE Venturing is the most commendable part of human Prudence.

Ibid., 245.

YOU can do very little with faith, but you can do nothing without it.

Samuel Butler, N, 336.

THERE is no strong performance without a little fanaticism in the performer.

Emerson, J, IX, 203.

A GREAT part of courage is the courage of having done the thing before.

Emerson, E, II, 263.

No great man ever complains of want of opportunity.

Ibid., J, V, 534.

IT is best for great Men to shoot over, and for lesser Men to shoot short.

Halifax, 245.

A MAN who is Master of Patience, is Master of everything else.

Ibid., 253.

PATIENCE is a most necessary qualification for business; many a man would rather you heard his story than granted his request.

Chesterfield, 573.

A CONSTANT smirk upon the face, and a whiffling activity of the body, are strong indications of futility. Whoever is in a hurry, shows that the thing he is about is too big for him.

Ibid., 231.

A MAN of sense may be in haste, but can never be in a hurry.

Ibid., 398.

IN skating over thin ice, our safety is in our speed.

Emerson, E, I, 127.

SUCCESS is the necessary misfortune of life, but it is only to the very unfortunate that it comes early.

Trollope, Orley Farm.

NOTHING makes a man so cross as success.
Trollope, Orley Farm.

OUR business in this world is not to succeed, but to continue to fail, in good spirits.
R. L. Stevenson, E, 84.

To travel hopefully is a better thing than to arrive.
Ibid., V, 178.

THE Secret of success in life is known only to those who have not succeeded.
Churton Collins, L, 316.

TAKE care to get what you like or you will be forced to like what you get.
Bernard Shaw, 242.

WE have all sinned and come short of the glory of making ourselves as comfortable as we easily might have done.
Samuel Butler, W, 82.

XXXIX

ENMITY, HATRED, REVENGE

NOTHING would more contribute to make a Man wise, than to have always an Enemy in his view.
Halifax, 255.

THOU mayest extract an Antidote out of a Viper, and good out of an Enemy. An Enemy will tell thee more truly of thy Imperfections than the best of Friends will adventure to do.
Dr. Fuller, II, 186.

MEN hate more steadily than they love; and if I have said something to hurt a man once, I shall not get the better of this by saying many things to please him.
Dr. Johnson, B, III, 150.

I AM willing to love all mankind, except an American.
Ibid., 290.

MEN who wish to inspire terror seem thereby to confess themselves cowards.
Emerson, E, III, 144.

SELDOM do people vex us on purpose, and yet prejudice very often makes us think that they do.
Bishop Wilson, S, 127.

MEN do not suspect faults which they do not commit.
Dr. Johnson, B, I, 288.

ALL country people hate each other. They have so little comfort that they envy their neighbours the smallest pleasure or advantage. . . . If you do anyone a favour, the whole neighbourhood is up in arms; the clamour is like that of a rookery.
Hazlitt, R T, II, 116

EVERYBODY knows that it is only necessary to raise a bugbear before the English imagination in order to govern it at will. Whatever they hate or fear, they implicitly believe in, merely from the scope it gives to these passions.

Hazlitt, B, III, 9.

IT does not matter much what a man hates provided he hates something.

Samuel Butler, N, 217.

VIOLENT antipathies are always suspicious, and betray a secret affinity

Hazlitt, T T, I, 377.

REVENGE is a kind of Wild Justice; which the more Man's Nature runs to, the more ought Law to weed it out.

Bacon, E, 13.

TOO many there be to whom a dead enemy smells well, and who find musk and amber in revenge.

Sir Thomas Browne, C, 103.

IT costs more to revenge than to bear with injuries.

Bishop Wilson, M, 75.

THE Memory and Conscience never did, nor never will agree about forgiving Injuries.

Halifax, 252.

XL

ANGER

To be angry, is to revenge the fault of others upon ourselves.

Pope, 287.

EVERY Stroke our Fury strikes is sure to hit ourselves at last.

Wm. Penn, 57.

ANGER is one of the sinews of the soul; he that wants it hath a maimed mind.

Thomas Fuller, H, 160.

ANGER raiseth Invention, but it overheateth the Oven.

Halifax, 237.

MALICE, like Lust, when it is at the Height, doth not know Shame.

Ibid., 239.

ANGER is never without an Argument, but seldom with a good one.

Ibid., 237.

WHEN a Man is very kind or very angry, there is no sure Guard but Silence upon that Subject.

Ibid., 246.

ACT nothing in furious Passion; it's putting to Sea in a Storm.

Dr. Fuller, I, 18.

OUR passions are like convulsion fits, which though they make us stronger for the time, leave us weaker ever after.

Pope, 287.

SUDDEN passion is called short-lived madness; it is
a madness indeed, but the fits of it return so often in
choleric people that it may well be called a continual
madness.

Chesterfield, 637.

OBSERVE a man in a passion, see his eyes glaring, his
face enflamed, his limbs trembling, and his tongue
stammering and faltering with rage, and then ask
yourself calmly whether upon any account you would
be that human wild-beast.

Ibid.

I NEVER saw, nor scarcely ever heard of, a Quaker
in a passion.   *Ibid.*

THE tigers of wrath are wiser than the horses of
instruction.   *Blake.*

DAMN braces.   Bless relaxes.   *Ibid.*

HALF anger and half confidence are the most imprudent things in the world.

Chesterfield, 901.

HE that fixes his attention on things always before
him will never have long cessations of anger.

Dr. Johnson, R, No. 112.

RESENTMENT gratifies him who intended an injury,
and pains him unjustly who did not intend it.

Ibid., B, IV, 367.

IT is too common for those who have unjustly suffered pain to inflict it likewise in their turn with the
same injustice.

Ibid., W, III, 294.

XLI

QUARRELS

IN any quarrel that person will generally be thought in the wrong, who it was foretold would quarrel.

Chesterfield, 1011.

THERE is no such test of a man's superiority of character as in the well-conducting of an unavoidable quarrel.

Sir Henry Taylor, S, 101.

WHEN we quarrel, how we wish we had been blameless!

Emerson, J, IX, 497.

THOSE who are the loudest and bitterest in their complaints of persecution and ill-usage are the first to provoke it. In the warfare waged so fondly and (as it is at last discovered) so unequally with the world, the assailants and the sufferers will be generally found to be the same persons.

Hazlitt, A, II, 262.

THE man who threatens the world is always ridiculous; for the world can easily go on without him, and in a short time will cease to miss him.

Dr. Johnson, W, IV, 58.

THOSE who are at war with others, are not at peace with themselves. It is the uneasiness, the turbulence, the acrimony within that recoils upon external objects.

Hazlitt, A, II, 231.

QUARRELS

THERE is a sort of man who goes through the world in a succession of quarrels, always able to make out that he is in the right, although he never ceases to put other men in the wrong.

Sir Henry Taylor, S, 103.

A MAN who is sure to cause injuries to be done to him wherever he goes, is almost as great an evil and inconvenience as if he were himself the wrong-doer.

Ibid.

XLII

ENVY

ENVY is almost the only vice which is practicable at all times, and in every place; the only passion which can never lie quiet from want of irritation.

Dr. Johnson, R, No. 183.

ENVY, among other ingredients, has a mixture of the love of justice in it. We are more angry at undeserved than at deserved good fortune.

Hazlitt, C, 6.

I THANK God I never was sensible of that dark and vile passion, except that formerly I have sometimes envied a successful rival with a fine woman.

Chesterfield, 1325.

ENVY is commonly reciprocal.

Dr. Johnson, W, XI, 50.

WE are all envious naturally; but by checking envy, we get the better of it.

Ibid., B, III, 271.

THERE is nothing more universally commended than a fine day; the reason is, that people can commend it without envy.

Shenstone, 214.

HAPPINESS is nothing if it is not known, and very little if it is not envied.

Dr. Johnson, Idler, No. 80.

HAPPINESS is not found in self-contemplation; it is perceived only when it is reflected from another.

Ibid., No. 41.

Envy is the sincerest form of flattery.

Churton Collins, E, 95.

Envy and fear are the only passions to which no pleasure is attached.

Ibid., 97.

XLIII

CALUMNY

CALUMNY differs from most other injuries in this dreadful circumstance. He who commits it never can repair it. A false report may spread where a recantation never reaches, and an accusation must certainly fly faster than a defence while the greater part of mankind are base and wicked. *Dr. Johnson, H,* 36.

DEFAMATION and calumny never attack where there is no weak place; they magnify, but they do not create.
Chesterfield, I, 307.

THERE is nothing that so much gratifies an ill tongue as when it finds an angry Heart.
Dr. Fuller, I, 199.

THERE are few who do not sometimes, in the wantonness of thoughtless mirth, or the heat of transient resentment, speak of their friends and benefactors with levity and contempt. *Dr. Johnson, W,* III, 256.

IN the case of scandal, as in that of robbery, the receiver is always thought as bad as the thief.
Chesterfield, 164.

SCANDAL is gossip made tedious by morality.
Oscar Wilde, 58

THE Man that despiseth Slander deserveth it.
Halifax, 255.

LIES

A MIXTURE of a Lie doth ever add Pleasure.

Bacon, E, 2.

TRUTH is beautiful. Without doubt; and so are lies.

Emerson, J, III, 437.

As universal a practice as lying is, and as easy one as it seems, I do not remember to have heard three good lies in all my conversation, even from those who were most celebrated in that faculty.

Swift, III, 411.

EQUIVOCATION is half-way to Lying, as Lying the whole way to Hell.

Wm. Penn, 36.

LIES and perfidy are the refuge of fools and cowards.

Chesterfield, 516.

THE greatest fools are the greatest liars. For my own part, I judge of every man's truth by his degree of understanding. *Ibid.,* 59.

A PERSON who does not tell lies will not believe that others tell them. From old habit, he cannot break the connection between words and things.

Hazlitt, W, XII, 220.

WEAK and impulsive people may be, and very often are, sincere, but they are seldom truthful.

Churton Collins, E, 96.

No man speaks the truth or lives a true life two minutes together.

Emerson, J, III, 455.

CONVERSATION

LANGUAGE most shows a man: Speak, that I may see thee.

Ben Jonson, 415.

THAT character in conversation which commonly passes for agreeable, is made up of civility and falsehood.

Pope, 300.

THE wonder we often express at our neighbours keeping dull company, would lessen if we reflected that most people seek companions less to be talked to, than to talk.

Ibid., 304.

IF thou hast a mind to get Esteem in Company, have the Art to edge about, till thou canst get into a subject thou has studied and art Master of.

Dr. Fuller, I, 59.

MAKE not thy own Person, Family, Relations or Affairs, the frequent Subject of thy Tattle. . . . Say not, In truth, I cannot allow of such a thing. My Manner and Custom is to do thus. I neither eat nor drink in a morning. I am apt to be troubled with Corns. My Child said such a Witty thing last night.

Ibid., 195.

WHEN one is relating anything, interrupt him not, unless there be great reason for it: Don't say, No, it was thus, but I'll tell you. You leave out the best Part of it, etc.

Ibid., 156.

IF thou art a Person that hast good Authority with the Company, 'twere good to look confidently, yet not scornfully, and then mildly say, "This is my Opinion."

Dr. Fuller, I, 190.

BEWARE of telling an improbable Truth.

Ibid., II, 124.

BE not extravagantly high in Expression of thy Commendations of Men thou likest: It may make the Hearers' Stomach rise.

Ibid., I, 51.

CONSTANT popping off of Proverbs will make thee a By-word thyself.

Ibid., 196.

AFTER thou has rallied and made thyself merry in Company, thou art no sooner gone out of it but they will examine thee from Head to Foot: And one that has not spoke a word while thou wert present, will tear thee with his Teeth.

Ibid., II, 167.

A MAN often repents that he has spoken, but seldom that he has held his Tongue.

Ibid., 90.

A MODESTY in delivering our sentiments leaves us a liberty of changing them without blushing.

Bishop Wilson, M, 127.

NEVER talk your best in the company of fools.

Chesterfield, 648.

THIS I will advise you to, which is, never to attack whole bodies of any kind. . . Individuals forgive sometimes; but bodies and societies never do.

Chesterfield, 32.

ALL general reflections upon nations and societies are the trite, threadbare jokes of those who set up for wit without having any. *Ibid.*

MANY people come into company full of what they intend to say in it themselves, without the least regard to others; and thus charged up to the muzzle are resolved to let it off at any rate. I knew a man who had a story about a gun, which he thought a good one and that he told it very well. He tried all means in the world to turn the conversation upon guns; but, if he failed in his attempt, he started in his chair, and said he heard a gun fired; but when the company assured him they heard no such thing, he answered, perhaps then I was mistaken; but however, since we are talking of guns,—and then told his story, to the great indignation of the company

Ibid., 647.

A MAN who tells nothing, or who tells all, will equally have nothing told him.

Ibid., 572.

THAT people should endeavour to excel in conversation, I do not wonder; because in conversation praise is instantly reverberated.

Dr. Johnson, B, V, 59.

THE man who talks to unburthen his mind is the man to delight you.

Ibid., III, 247.

175

THAT is the happiest conversation where there is no competition, no vanity, but a calm quiet interchange of sentiments.

Dr. Johnson, B, II, 359.

BUT, Sir, may there not be very good conversation without a contest for superiority?

No animated conversation, Sir.

Ibid., 444.

WHOEVER thinks of going to bed before twelve o'clock is a scoundrel.

Ibid., M, II, 19.

IT is always observable that silence propagates itself, and that the longer talk has been suspended, the more difficult it is to find anything to say.

Ibid., A, No. 84.

THERE are not many situations more incessantly uneasy than that in which the man is placed who is watching an opportunity to speak, without courage to take it.

Ibid., R, No. 157.

No man speaks concerning another, even suppose it be in his praise, if he thinks he does not hear him, exactly as he would, if he thought he was within hearing.   *Ibid., B*, IV, 32.

ABSENT he is a character understood, but present he is a force respected.

Santayana, P, 273.

I NEVER desire to converse with a man who has written more than he has read.

Dr. Johnson, M, II, 6.

THE conversation of authors is not so good as might be imagined; but, such as it is (and with rare exceptions) it is better than any other.

Hazlitt, P S, I, 62.

IT is a very bad sign (unless where it arises from singular modesty) when you cannot tell a man's profession from his conversation. Such persons either feel no interest in what concerns them most, or do not express what they feel.

Ibid., R T, II, 30.

WE are cold to others only when we are dull in ourselves.

Ibid., L R, II, 197.

THE most silent people are generally those who think most highly of themselves. They fancy themselves superior to every one else; and not being sure of making good their secret pretensions, decline entering the lists altogether.

Ibid., C, 38.

WE talk little, if we do not talk about ourselves.

Ibid., 67.

AN indigestion is an excellent commonplace for two people that never met before.

Ibid., L R, II, 204.

WE may be willing to tell a story twice, never to hear one more than once.

Ibid., C, 87.

THOSE who can keep secrets, have no curiosity. We only wish to gain knowledge, that we may impart it.

Ibid., W, XI, 543.

"I never offered an opinion till I was sixty," said the old Turk; "and then it was one which had been in our family for a century."

Disraeli, Iskander, Chap. VIII.

Seeing we are civilized Englishmen, let us not be naked savages in our talk.

Thomas Fuller, H, 145.

Intemperance in talk makes a dreadful havoc in the heart.

Bishop Wilson, M, 157.

Watch your own speech, and notice how it is guided by your less conscious purposes.

George Eliot, Mill on the Floss.

Sir, people may come to do anything almost, by talking of it.

Dr. Johnson, B, V, 286.

The conversation of men is a mixture of regrets and apprehensions.

Emerson, E, IV, 189.

Don't *say* things. What you *are* stands over you the while, and thunders so that I cannot hear what you say to the contrary. *Ibid.*, III, 233.

The habit of common and continuous speech is a symptom of mental deficiency. It proceeds from not knowing what is going on in other people's minds.

Bagehot, L, I, 47

Conversation is an art in which a man has all mankind for his competitors.

Emerson, E, II, 336.

THERE can be no fairer ambition than to excel in talk.

R. L. Stevenson, M, 144.

THE first duty of a man is to speak; that is his chief business in this world.

Ibid., 146.

ALL natural talk is a festival of ostentation; and by the laws of the game each accepts and fans the vanity of the other.

Ibid., 149.

LITERATURE in many of its branches is no other than the shadow of good talk.

Ibid., 145.

XLVI

WIT

SOME Men have acted Courage who had it not; but no Man can act Wit, if Nature doth not teach him his Part. True Wit is always revenged upon any false Pretender that meddleth with it.

Halifax, 250.

LET not thy jests, like mummy, be made of dead men's flesh. Abuse not any that are departed; for, to wrong their memories, is to rob their ghosts of their winding-sheets.

Thomas Fuller, H, 146.

MOCK not a cobbler for his black thumbs.

Ibid.

WIT is so shining a quality that everybody admires it; most people aim at it, all people fear it, and few love it unless in themselves.

Chesterfield, 638.

A WIT is a very unpopular denomination, as it carries terror along with it; and people in general are as much afraid of a live wit in company as a woman is of a gun, which she thinks may go off of itself, and do her a mischief.

Ibid., 157.

IF God gives you wit ... wear it like your sword in the scabbard, and do not brandish it to the terror of the whole company.

Ibid., 638.

A WISE man will live as much within his wit as his income.   *Ibid.*, 639.

WIT

LEARN to shrink yourself to the size of the company you are in.

Chesterfield, 639.

EVERY man has some time in his life an ambition to be a wag.

Dr. Johnson, B, IV, 2.

THOSE who cannot miss an opportunity of saying a good thing . . . are not to be trusted with the management of any great question.

Hazlitt, C, 59.

BEWARE of jokes; . . . we go away hollow and ashamed.

Emerson, E, III, 233.

XLVII

LAUGHTER

Sudden Glory is the passion which maketh those Grimaces called Laughter; and is caused either by some sudden act of their own, that pleaseth them; or by the apprehension of some deformed thing in another, by comparison whereof they suddenly applaud themselves.

Hobbes, 27.

'Tis a good thing to laugh at any rate; and if a straw can tickle a man, it is an instrument of happiness.

Dryden, II, 133.

We seldom ever laugh without crime.

Bishop Wilson, *M*, 96.

He who laughs, and is himself ridiculous, bears a double share of Ridicule.

Shaftesbury, I, 83.

Were it not for Bunglers in the manner of doing it, hardly any Man would ever find out he was laughed at.

Halifax, 251.

Men have been wise in very different modes; but they have always laughed the same way.

Dr. Johnson, *W*, II, 45.

A coarse nature still betrays itself in his contemptible squeals of joy.

Emerson, *E*, III, 227.

The vulgar often laugh, but never smile; whereas well-bred people often smile, but seldom laugh. A witty thing never excited laughter; it pleases only the mind, and never distorts the countenance.

Chesterfield, 637.

LAUGHTER

I AM sure that, since I have had the full use of my reason, nobody has ever heard me laugh.

Chesterfield, 94.

I HATE scarce smiles; I love laughing.

Blake, L, I, 62.

XLVIII

DISPUTES

DISPUTES upon any subject are a sort of trial of the understanding, and must end in the mortification of one or other of the disputants.

Chesterfield, 633.

A DISPUTE begun in jest, upon a subject which a moment before was on both parts regarded with careless indifference, is continued by the desire of conquest, till vanity kindles into rage, and opposition rankles into enmity. Against this hasty mischief I know not what security can be obtained.

Dr. Johnson, Idler, No. 23.

WE are not satisfied to be right, unless we can prove others to be quite wrong.

Hazlitt, N, 236.

TREATING your adversary with respect is giving him an advantage to which he is not entitled.

Dr. Johnson, B, V, 29.

A GOOD life is a main argument.

Ben Jonson, 391.

PEOPLE hate those who make them feel their own inferiority.

Chesterfield, 337.

WHEREVER the truth is injured, defend it.

Emerson, J, III, 269.

BUT, Sir, truth will always bear an examination. Yes, Sir, but it is painful to be forced to defend it.

Dr. Johnson, B, III, 11.

A MAN may be in as just possession of Truth as of a City, and yet be forced to surrender.

Sir Thomas Browne, R, 10.

MEN may be convinced, but they cannot be pleased, against their will.

Dr. Johnson, W, III, 159.

THERE is a danger in being persuaded before one understands.

Bishop Wilson, M, 109.

WHEN a thing ceases to be a subject of controversy, it ceases to be a subject of interest.

Hazlitt, W, XII, 384.

THE only sin which we never forgive in each other is difference of opinion. We know beforehand that yonder man must think as we do. Has he not two hands,—two feet,—hair and nails? Does he not eat, —bleed,—laugh,—cry? His dissent from me is the veriest affectation. This conclusion is at once the logic of persecution and of love. And the ground of our indignation is our conviction that his dissent is some wilfulness he practises on himself. He checks the flow of his opinion, as the cross cow holds up her milk. Yes, and we look into his eye, and see that he knows it, and hides his eye from ours.

Emerson, E, III, 124.

XLIX

THE RICH AND GREAT

A DIFFERENCE of opinion, though in the merest trifles, alienates little minds, especially of high rank. . . . It is impossible to inform, but very easy to displease them.

Chesterfield, 575.

GREAT lords and great ladies don't love to have their mouths stopped.

Dr. Johnson, B., IV, 116.

BY that time Men are fit for Company, they see the Objections to it.

Halifax, 243.

THE difference between what is commonly called ordinary company and good company is only hearing the same things said in a little room or in a large salon, at small tables or at great tables, before two candles or twenty sconces.

Pope, 294.

HIS scorn of the great is repeated too often to be real; no man thinks much of that which he despises.

Dr. Johnson, W, IV, 99.

MRS. Montagu has dropt me. Now, Sir, there are people whom one should like very well to drop, but would not wish to be dropt by.

Ibid., B, IV, 73.

HIGH people, Sir, are the best.

Ibid., III, 353.

PRETEND not thou to scorn the Pomp of the world before thou knowest it.

Dr. Fuller, I, 56.

IF thou art cheated by a great Man, lose thy Money, and say nothing.

Ibid., 19.

IF every man who wears a laced coat (that he can pay for) was extirpated, who would miss them?

Dr. Johnson, M, I, 253.

SIR, it is a great thing to dine with the Canons of Christ Church.

Ibid., B, II, 445.

PEOPLE in high life are hardened to the wants and distresses of mankind as surgeons are to their bodily pains.

Chesterfield, 412.

ONE who would thrive by seeking favours from the great, should never trouble them for small ones.

Sir Henry Taylor, S, 97.

NEVER claim as a right what you can ask as a favour.

Churton Collins, E, 98.

WE honour the rich, because they have externally the freedom, power, and grace which we feel to be proper to man, proper to us.

Emerson, E, I, 3.

IT is perhaps a more fortunate destiny to have a taste for collecting shells than to be born a millionaire.

R. L. Stevenson, E, 37.

SIR, the insolence of wealth will creep out.
Dr. Johnson, B, III, 316.

IT is not given to the children of men to be philosophers without envy.   Lookers-on can hardly bear the spectacle of the great world.

Bagehot, L, II, 286.

MOST Lords are feeble and forlorn.
Ibid., E, 122.

MAN is the only animal which esteems itself rich in proportion to the number and voracity of its parasites.
Bernard Shaw, 234.

AH! if the rich were rich as the poor fancy riches!
Emerson, E, I, 292.

L

FASHION

WHEN a man is once in fashion all he does is right.
Chesterfield, 562.

I WOULD rather have you a fop than a sloven.
Ibid., 246.

WEAR good Clothes: they open all Doors to us.
Dr. Fuller, I, 87.

NEVER be the first nor the last in the fashion.
Chesterfield, 632.

ALL such dresses are forbidden, which incite irregular
desires.
Bishop Wilson, M, 6.

POETS, artists, and men of genius in general, are
seldom coxcombs, but often slovens; for they find
something out of themselves better worth studying
than their own persons.
Hazlitt, P S, I, 399.

FASHION is like God, man cannot see into its holy of
holies and live.
Samuel Butler, N, 226.

FOR an idea ever to be fashionable is ominous, since
it must afterwards be always old-fashioned.
Santayana, W, 55.

FASHION is gentility running away from vulgarity,
and afraid of being overtaken.
Hazlitt, N, 264.

LI

VULGARITY

VULGARITY is an inadequate conception of the art of living.

Bishop Creighton, L.

THE essence of all vulgarity lies in want of sensation.

Ruskin, Sesame and Lilies.

IF a person has no delicacy, he has you in his power.

Hazlitt, L R, II, 258.

BARBARISM and rusticity may perhaps be instructed, but false refinement is incorrigible.

Ibid., B, I, 439.

A NICE man is a man of nasty ideas.

Swift, III, 409.

IT is the test of reason and refinement to be able to subsist without bugbears.

Hazlitt, W, XII, 465.

LII

VANITY AND PRIDE

VANITY is the Mother, and Affectation is the Darling Daughter; Vanity is the Sin, and Affectation is the Punishment; the first may be called the Root of Self-Love, the other the Fruit.

Halifax, 38.

EVERYBODY hath not Wit enough to Act out of Interest, but everybody hath little enough to do it out of Vanity.

Ibid., 241.

MUCH of the pain and pleasure of mankind arises from the conjectures which every one makes of the thoughts of others; we all enjoy praise which we do not hear, and resent contempt which we do not see.

Dr. Johnson, Idler, No. 103.

THERE is a Degree of Vanity that recommendeth; if it goeth further, it exposeth.

So much as to stir the Blood do commendable Things, but not so much as to possess the Brain, and turn it round.

Halifax, 241.

IT is not to be imagined by how many different ways vanity defeats its own purposes.

Chesterfield, 343.

VANITY is the more odious and shocking to everybody, because everybody, without exception, has vanity; and two vanities can never love one another.

Ibid., 646.

To this principle of vanity, which philosophers call a mean one, and which I do not, I owe great part of the figure which I have made in life.

Chesterfield, 562.

HE whose own worth doth speak, need not speak his own worth. . . . Only anchorets, that want company, may crown themselves with their own commendations.

Thomas Fuller, H, 147.

EVERY other enjoyment malice may destroy; every other panegyric envy may withhold; but no human power can deprive the boaster of his own encomiums.

Dr. Johnson, R, No. 193.

ALL censure of a man's self is oblique praise.

Ibid., B, III, 323.

THERE is in human nature a general inclination to make people stare; and every wise man has himself to cure of it, and does cure himself.

Ibid., B, II, 74.

EVERY man has a lurking wish to appear considerable in his native place.

Ibid., 141.

No man sympathizes with the sorrows of vanity.

Ibid., W, IV, 53.

YOU must never seem to affect the character in which you have a mind to shine. Modesty is the only sure bait when you angle for praise.

Chesterfield, 344.

HE who loves praise, loves temptation.

Bishop Wilson, M, 114.

EVERY man has a right to be conceited until he is successful.

Disraeli, The Young Duke.

To be vain is rather a mark of humility than pride.

Swift, III, 405.

WHOEVER desires the character of a proud man, ought to conceal his vanity.

Ibid.

PRIDE is as loud a Beggar as Want, and a great deal more Saucy.

Halifax, 181.

GREAT Bashfulness is oftener an Effect of Pride than of Modesty.

Ibid., 245.

No cause more frequently produces bashfulness than too high an opinion of our own importance.

Dr. Johnson, R, No. 159.

HE who thinks his Place below him, will certainly be below his Place.

Halifax, 182.

THE passions grafted on wounded pride are the most inveterate; they are green and vigorous in old age.

Santayana, E, 22.

THOUGH pride is not a virtue, it is the parent of many virtues.

Churton Collins, E, 100.

PRIDE is handsome, economical; pride eradicates so many vices, letting none subsist but itself, that it seems as if it were a great gain to exchange vanity for pride. Pride can go without domestics, without fine clothes, can live in a house with two rooms, can eat potato, purslain, beans, lyed corn, can work on the soil, can travel afoot, can talk with poor men, or sit silent well contented in fine saloons. But vanity costs money, labour, horses, men, women, health and peace, and is still nothing at last, a long way leading nowhere. Only one drawback: proud people are intolerably selfish, and the vain are gentle and giving.

Emerson, E, II, 249.

LIII

THE ART OF PLEASING

MOST arts require long study and application; but the most useful art of all, that of pleasing, requires only the desire.

Chesterfield, 576.

IF you will please people, you must please them in their own way.

Ibid., 286.

WHAT pleases you in others will in general please them in you.

Ibid., 355.

THE art of pleasing consists in being pleased.

Hazlitt, R T, I, 115.

The excessive Desire of Pleasing goes along almost always with the Apprehension of not being liked.

Dr. Fuller, II, 178.

THE greatest mistake is the trying to be more agreeable than you can be.

Bagehot, B, 294.

DEFERENCE is the most complicate, the most indirect, and the most elegant of all compliments.

Shenstone, 254.

MORAL qualities rule the world, but at short distances, the senses are despotic.

Emerson, E, I, 274.

GOOD manners are made up of petty sacrifices.

Ibid., III, 238.

OUR Manners, like our Faces, though ever so beautiful, must differ in their Beauty.

Shaftesbury, III, 262.

EVERYONE thinks himself well-bred.

Ibid., I, 65.

POLITENESS . . . is fictitious benevolence

Dr. Johnson, B, V, 82.

POLITENESS is one of those advantages which we never estimate rightly but by the inconvenience of its loss.

Ibid., R, No. 98.

THE difference between a well-bred, and an ill-bred man is this: One immediately attracts your liking, and the other your aversion. You love the one till you find reason to hate him; you hate the other till you find reason to love him.

Ibid., B, IV, 319.

THERE are ten genteel women for one genteel man, because they are more restrained. A man without some degree of restraint is insufferable; but we are all less restrained than women. Were a woman sitting in company to put out her legs before her as most men do, we should be tempted to kick them in.

Ibid., III, 53.

EVERY man of any education would rather be called a rascal than accused of deficiency in the graces.

Ibid., 54.

SIR, I look upon myself as a very polite man.

Ibid., V, 363.

LIV

FLATTERY

A CONTINUAL feast of commendation is only to be attained by merit or by wealth.

Dr. Johnson, R, No. 193.

WHEN he whom everybody else flatters, flatters me, I then am truly happy.

Ibid., B, II, 227.

JUST praise is only a debt, but flattery is a present.

Ibid., R, No. 155.

YOU think I love flattery, and so I do; but a little too much always disgusts me: that fellow Richardson, on the contrary, could not be contented to sail quietly down the stream of reputation, without longing to taste the froth from every stroke of the oar.

Ibid., M, I, 273.

WHO forbears to flatter an author or a lady?

Ibid., W, II, 256.

THE applause of a single human being is of great consequence.

Ibid., B, IV, 32.

WE thirst for approbation, yet cannot forgive the approver.

Emerson, E, I, 164.

PRAISE is like ambergris: a little whiff of it, and by snatches, is very agreeable; but when a man holds a whole lump of it to your nose, it is a stink, and strikes you down.

Pope, 302.

Love of flattery in most men proceeds from the mean opinion they have of themselves; in women from the contrary.

Swift, III, 408.

Women who are either indisputably beautiful, or indisputably ugly, are best flattered upon the score of their understandings.

Chesterfield, 142.

I recommended to you in my last an innocent piece of art—that of flattering people behind their backs, in presence of those who, to make their own court, much more than for your sake, will not fail to repeat, and even amplify, the praise to the party concerned. This is, of all flattery, the most pleasing, and consequently the most effectual.

Ibid., 212.

Though compliments should arise naturally out of the occasion, they should not appear to be prompted by the spur of it; for then they seem hardly spontaneous. Applaud a man's speech at the moment when he sits down, and he will take your compliment as exacted by the demands of common civility; but let some space intervene, and then show him that the merits of his speech have dwelt with you when you might have been expected to have forgotten them, and he will remember your compliment for a much longer time than you have remembered his speech.

Sir Henry Taylor, S, 237.

It is a grace in flattery so to let fall your compliments as that you shall seem to consider them to be a matter of indifference to him to whom they are addressed.

Ibid.

But the mode of flattery which, being at once safe and efficacious, is the best adapted to the purposes of a statesman, is the flattery of *listening*. He that can wear the appearance of drinking in every word that is said with thirsty ears, possesses such a faculty for conciliating mankind as a syren might envy.

Sir Henry Taylor, S, 238.

No syren did ever so charm the ear of the listener, as the listening ear has charmed the soul of the syren.

Ibid., 239.

These, however, are merely the *tricks* of statesmanship, which it may be quite as well to despise as to practise.

Ibid., 240.

LV

CEREMONY

CEREMONY keeps up all things.

Selden, 24.

OF all people, ladies have no cause to cry down ceremonies, for they take themselves extremely slighted without it. And were they not used with ceremony, with compliments and addresses, with legs, and kissing of hands, they were the pitifullest creatures in the world.

Ibid., 25.

ALL ceremonies are in themselves very silly things.

Chesterfield, 506.

CEREMONY is the superstition of good-breeding, as well as of religion; but yet, being an outwork to both, should not be absolutely demolished.

Ibid., W, II, 285.

AN age of ignorance is an age of ceremony.

Dr. Johnson, W, X, 393.

THE compliments and ceremonies of our breeding should recall, however remotely, the grandeur of our destiny.

Emerson, E, I, 274.

LVI

KINGS AND COURTS

It is a miserable State of Mind, to have few Things to desire, and many Things to fear: and yet that commonly is the Case of Kings.

Bacon, E, 65.

King James said to the fly, Have I three kingdoms, and thou must needs fly into my eye?

Selden, 116.

Kings most commonly, though strong in Legions, are but weak at Arguments.

Milton, II, 443.

A Prince without letters is a Pilot without eyes.

Ben Jonson, 405.

They say Princes learn no art truly, but the art of horsemanship. The reason is, the brave beast is no flatterer. He will throw a Prince as soon as his Groom.   *Ibid.*

The penetration of Princes seldom goes deeper than the surface. It is the exterior that always engages their hearts; and I would never advise you to give yourself much trouble about their understandings.

Chesterfield, 272.

When a Prince trusteth a Man with a dangerous Secret, he would not be sorry to hear the Bell toll for him.

Halifax, 215.

A Prince who will not undergo the Difficulty of Understanding, must undergo the Danger of Trusting.

Ibid., 214.

A COUNTRY governed by a despot is an inverted cone.

Dr. Johnson, B, III, 283.

VULGARITY in a king flatters the majority of the nation.

Bernard Shaw, 228.

MEN at Court think so much of their own Cunning that they forget other Men's.

Halifax, 228.

THE Court may be said to be a Company of well-bred fashionable Beggars.

Ibid.

AT Court, people embrace without acquaintance, serve one another without friendship, and injure one another without hatred. Interest, not sentiment, is the growth of that soil.

Chesterfield, 575.

LVII

POWER

MEN in Great Place are thrice Servants: Servants of the Sovereign or State; Servants of Fame; and Servants of Business. So as they have no Freedom; neither in their Persons, nor in their Actions, nor in their Times.
Bacon, E, 34.

CERTAINLY Great Persons had need to borrow other Men's Opinions, to think themselves happy; for if they judge by their own Feeling, they cannot find it: But if they think with themselves, what other men think of them, and that other men would fain be as they are, then they are happy, as it were by report.
Ibid., 35.

THERE are hardly two Creatures of a more differing Species than the same Man, when he is pretending to a Place, and when he is in possession of it.
Halifax, 228.

SOME Places have such a corrupting Influence upon the Man, that it is a supernatural thing to resist it.
Ibid.

THE Dependence of a great Man upon a greater is a Subjection that lower Men cannot easily comprehend.
Ibid., 231.

VERY shining Ministers, like the sun, are apt to scorch, when they shine the brightest.
Chesterfield, 1089.

How many are raised to high posts in the Church by the instigation of the devil, that their fall may be more dismal! *Bishop Wilson, M,* I.

THE opinion of having power often procures power.
Chesterfield, 1408.

THERE are few minds to which tyranny is not delightful.

Dr. Johnson, L, II, 110.

THE lust of government is the greatest lust.
Harrington, 469.

MAN is a toad-eating animal. The admiration of power in others is as common to man as the love of it in himself; the one makes him a tyrant, the other a slave.
Hazlitt, P E, 163.

POWER without love hath a terrifying aspect, and the Worship which is paid to it is like that which the Indians give out of fear to Wild Beasts and Devils.
Halifax, 57.

POWER is always gradually stealing away from the many to the few, because the few are more vigilant and consistent.

Dr. Johnson, A, No. 45.

THE imbecility of men is always inviting the impudence of power.

Emerson, E, I, 365.

YOU shall have joy, or you shall have power, said God; you shall not have both

Ibid., J, VI, 282.

THERE is no tyranny so hateful as a vulgar and anonymous tyranny. It is all-permeating, all-thwarting; it blasts every budding novelty and sprig of genius with its omnipresent and fierce stupidity. Such a headless people has the mind of a worm and the claws of a dragon. Anyone would be a hero who should quell the monster.

Santayana, R, II, 127.

DEMOCRACY becomes a government of bullies tempered by editors.

Emerson, J, VII, 193.

LVIII

LIBERTY

THO' the laziness of a slavish subjection hath its Charms for the more gross and earthly part of Mankind, yet to men made of a better sort of Clay, all that the world can give without Liberty hath no taste.

Halifax, 62.

LIBERTY is the Mistress of Mankind, she hath powerful Charms which do so dazzle us that we find Beauties in her which perhaps are not there, as we do in other Mistresses; yet if she was not a Beauty, the World would not run mad for her.

Ibid.

LIBERTY can neither be got, nor kept, but by so much Care, that Mankind are generally unwilling to give the Price for it.

Ibid., 224.

LIBERTY is short and fleeting, a transient grace that lights upon the earth by stealth and at long intervals; . . . but power is eternal.

Hazlitt, P E, 314.

LIBERTY means responsibility. That is why most men dread it.

Bernard Shaw, 229.

WHEN the People contend for their Liberty, they seldom get anything by their Victory but new Masters.

Halifax, 224.

THE people are deceived by names, but not by things.

Harrington, 483.

THE people cannot see, but they can feel.
Harrington, 483.

THEY who have put out the people's eyes, reproach them of their blindness.
Milton, I, 192.

THE notion of liberty amuses the people of England, and helps to keep off the *taedium vitae*. When a butcher tells you that his heart bleeds for his country, he has, in fact, no uneasy feeling.
Dr. Johnson, B, I, 394.

IT has been observed, that they who most loudly clamour for liberty do not most liberally grant it.
Ibid., W, II, 144.

LIX

POLITICS

THE body of a man, not actuated or led by the soul, is a dead thing out of pain and misery; but the body of a people, not actuated or led by the soul of government, is a living thing in pain and misery.

Harrington, 469.

STATE-BUSINESS is a cruel Trade; Good-nature is a Bungler in it.

Halifax, 217.

'TIS not juggling that is to be blamed, but much juggling, for the world cannot be governed without it.

Selden, 60.

LET the People think they Govern and they will be Governed.

Wm. Penn, 67.

POLITICIANS neither love nor hate. Interest, not sentiment, directs them.

Chesterfield, 900.

POPULARITY is a Crime from the Moment it is sought; it is only a Virtue where Men have it whether they will or no.

Halifax, 232.

No man can make a fortune or a figure in this country, without speaking, and speaking well, in public.

Chesterfield, 354.

MOST people have ears, but few have judgment; tickle those ears, and, depend upon it, you will catch their judgments, such as they are.

Ibid., 288.

To govern mankind one must not overrate them; and to please an audience as a speaker, one must not over-value it. When I first came into the House of Commons, I respected that assembly as a venerable one, and felt a certain awe upon me; but upon better acquaintance that awe soon vanished, and I discovered that of the five hundred and sixty, not above thirty could understand reason; . . . that those thirty only required plain common sense, dressed up in good language; and that all the others only required flowing and harmonious periods, whether they conveyed any meaning or not; having ears to hear, but not sense enough to judge.

Chesterfield, 604.

WE all know what Parliament is, and we are all ashamed of it.

R. L. Stevenson, E, 115.

A PARLIAMENT is nothing less than a big meeting of more or less idle people.

Bagehot, E, 180.

A CONSTITUTIONAL statesman is in general a man of common opinions and uncommon abilities.

Ibid., B, 2.

NINE-TENTHS of mankind are more afraid of violence than of anything else; and inconsistent moderation is always popular, because of all qualities it is most oppo-site to violence.

Ibid., 193.

EVERY numerous assembly is *mob,* let the individuals who compose it be what they will. . . . Understanding they have collectively none; but they have ears and eyes, which must be flattered and seduced.

Chesterfield, 418.

IT is the lot of every man who has to speak for the satisfaction of the crowd, that he must often speak in virtue of yesterday's faith, hoping it will come back to-morrow.

George Eliot, Romola.

THE tumultuous love of the populace must be seized and enjoyed in its first transports; there is no hoarding it to use upon occasions; it will not keep.

Chesterfield, 623.

THE giddy favour of a mutining Rout is as dangerous as their Fury.

Milton, I, 39.

IF ever the multitude deviate into the right, it is always for the wrong reason.

Chesterfield, 1431.

THERE is a Soul in that great body of the People, which may for a time be drowsy and unactive, but when the Leviathan is roused, it moveth like an angry Creature, and will neither be convinced nor resisted.

Halifax, 101.

THE angry Buzz of a Multitude is one of the bloodiest Noises in the World.

Ibid., 219.

THERE is an accumulative Cruelty in a number of Men, though none in particular are ill-natured.

Ibid.

PARTY is the madness of many, for the gain of a few.

Pope, 284.

THE best Party is but a kind of Conspiracy against the rest of the Nation.

Halifax, 225.

IGNORANCE maketh most Men go into a Party, and Shame keepeth them from getting out of it.

Ibid., 227.

WHEN great questions end, little parties begin.

Bagehot, E, 261.

SIR, you are a young man, but I have seen a great deal of the world, and take it upon my word and experience, that where you see a Whig you see a rascal.

Dr. Johnson, M, II, 393.

THE first Whig was the Devil.

Ibid., B, III, 326.

PATRIOTISM is the last refuge of a scoundrel.

Ibid., II, 348.

FACTION seldom leaves a man honest, however it might find him.

Ibid., W, II, 104.

I WOULD not give half a guinea to live under one form of government rather than another. It is of no moment to the happiness of an individual.

Ibid., B, II, 170.

So, Sir, you laugh at schemes of political improvement.
   Why, Sir, most schemes of political improvement are very laughable things.

Ibid., 102.

Iᴛ is the good of public life that it supplies agreeable topics and general conversation.

Dr. Johnson, L, I, 343.

Aғᴛᴇʀ all, there is such a thing as public good, though in general people seem not to think so.

Chesterfield, 1142.

As the Births of Living Creatures at first are ill-shapen, so are all Innovations, which are the Births of Time.

Bacon, E, 86.

Iғ mankind had wished for what is right, they might have had it long ago.

Hazlitt, P S, I, 325.

O Reason! when will thy long minority expire?

Ibid., L R, II, 453.

Iᴛ is essential to the triumph of reform that it should never succeed.

Ibid., W, XII, 213.

Eᴠᴇʀʏ reform is only a mask under cover of which a more terrible reform, which dares not yet name itself, advances.

Emerson, J, VII, 205.

As soon as Men have Understanding enough to find a Fault, they have enough to see the danger of mending it.

Halifax, 244.

I ᴀᴍ by education and conviction inclined to republicanism and puritanism. In America they have both; but I confess I feel a little staggered . . . when I ask myself, "Can they throughout the United States, from Boston to Baltimore, produce a single head like one of Titian's Venetian nobles, nurtured in all the pride of aristocracy and all the blindness of popery?" Of all the branches of political economy, the human face is perhaps the best criterion of *value*.

Hazlitt, W, XII, 377.

THE higher society is lifted the lower the individual may fall.

Bishop Creighton, MS.

THOSE who are fond of setting things to rights, have no great objection to seeing them wrong.

Hazlitt, C, 148.

THE most melancholy of human reflections, perhaps, is that, on the whole, it is a question whether the benevolence of mankind does most good or harm.

Bagehot, P, 188.

No people do so much harm as those who go about doing good.

Bishop Creighton, L.

IT is wonderful how little mischief we can do with all our trouble.

Ibid.

IT is better that ten Drones be fed than one Bee be famished.

Thomas Fuller, W, 33.

THE worst of charity is, that the lives you are asked to preserve are not worth preserving.

Emerson, E, II, 324.

To educate the wise man, the State exists; and with the appearance of the wise man, the State expires.

Emerson, E, I, 316.

THE irrational in the human has something about it altogether repulsive and terrible, as we see in the maniac, the miser, the drunkard, or the ape. A barbaric civilization, built on blind impulse and ambition, should fear to awaken a deeper detestation than could ever be aroused by those more beautiful tyrannies, chivalrous or religious, against which past revolutions have been directed.

Santayana, V.

DOES any thoughtful man suppose that . . . the present experiment in civilization is the last the world will see?

Ibid., R, II, 127.

LX

LAW

MEN are not hanged for stealing Horses, but that Horses may not be stolen.

Halifax, 229.

COMMONLY physicians, like beer, are best when they are old; and lawyers, like bread, when they are young and new.

Thomas Fuller, H, 50.

IF the Laws could speak for themselves, they would complain of the Lawyers in the first Place.

Halifax, 224.

EVERY actual State is corrupt. Good men must not obey the laws too well.

Emerson, E, I, 311.

As manners make laws, manners likewise repeal them.

Dr. Johnson, B, II, 419.

THE law is the last result of human wisdom acting upon human experience for the benefit of the public.

Ibid., M, I, 223.

LXI

LEARNING

THE Government of the World is a great thing; but it is a very coarse one, too, compared with the Fineness of Speculative Knowledge.

Halifax, 231.

BUSINESS is so much lower a thing than Learning, that a Man used to the last cannot easily bring his Stomach down to the first.

Ibid.

THE struggling for Knowledge hath a Pleasure in it like that of Wrestling with a fine Woman.

Ibid., 249.

No man is the wiser for his learning.

Selden, 70.

SOME people will never learn anything, for this reason, because they understand everything too soon.

Pope, 292.

SINCE you desire . . . an establishment in England, what do you think of being Greek Professor at one of our Universities? It is a very pretty sinecure, and requires very little knowledge (much less than, I hope, you have already) of that language.

Chesterfield, 80.

GREEK, Sir, is like lace; every man gets as much of it as he can.

Dr. Johnson, B, IV, 23.

LEARNING

THE good of Greek, in the last resort, is that it gives, in a way that nothing else quite does, the highest kind of joy; and such joys are not so common that we can afford to cast them away.

Mackail, C, 53.

EVERY man thinks meanly of himself for not having been a soldier, or not having been at sea.

Dr. Johnson, B, III, 265.

A CLERGYMAN, or a doctor, or a lawyer, feels himself no whit disgraced if he reaches the end of his worldly labours without special note or honour. But to a soldier or a sailor, such indifference to his merit is wormwood. It is the bane of the professions. Nine men out of ten who go into it must live discontented, and die disappointed.

Trollope, The Three Clerks.

No man forgets his original trade: the rights of nations, and of kings, sink into questions of grammar, if grammarians discuss them.

Dr. Johnson, W, II, 106.

THE vacant skull of a pedant generally furnishes out a throne and a temple for vanity.

Shenstone, 268.

THERE is often found in commentators a spontaneous strain of invective and contempt, more eager and venomous than is vented by the most furious controvertist in politics against those whom he is hired to defame.

Dr. Johnson, W, IX, 288.

Housmon?

HE who is not in some measure a pedant, though he may be a wise, cannot be a very happy man.

Hazlitt, R T, II, 28.

A SCHOOLMASTER should have an atmosphere of awe, and walk wonderingly, as if he was amazed at being himself.

Bagehot, L, I, 52.

KNOWLEDGE is of two kinds. We know a subject ourselves, or we know when we can find information upon it.

Dr. Johnson, B, II, 365.

I FEEL the reasonableness of what the lawyer or merchant or labourer has to allege against readers and thinkers, until I look at each of their wretched industries, and find them without end of aim.

Emerson, J, IX, 155.

LXII

LITERATURE

WORDS are the only things that last for ever.
                                        Hazlitt, T T, I, 250.

PEOPLE do not deserve to have good writing, they are
so pleased with bad.
                                        Emerson, J, VI, 132.

LANGUAGE put to its best purpose, used at its utmost
power and with the greatest skill, and recorded that it
may not pass away, evaporate and be forgotten, is what
we call, for want of a better word, literature.
                                        Mackail, C, 214.

LITERATURE is the effort of man to indemnify himself
for the wrongs of his condition.
                                        Emerson, E, IV, 137.

LITERATURE has its piety, its conscience; it cannot long
forget, without forfeiting all dignity, that it serves a
burdened and perplexed creature, a human animal
struggling to persuade the universal Sphinx to propose
a more intelligible riddle.
                                        Santayana, E, 138.

To turn events into ideas is the function of literature.
                                        Ibid.

GOOD writing is a kind of skating which carries off the
performer where he would not go.
                                        Emerson, J, VII, 334.

THE images of men's wits and knowledges remain in
books, exempted from the wrong of time, and capable
of perpetual renovation.
                                        Bacon, A, 90.

NEITHER are they fitly to be called images, because they generate still, and cast their seeds in the minds of others, provoking and causing infinite actions and opinions in succeeding ages: so that, if the invention of the ship was thought so noble, which carrieth riches and commodities from place to place, and consociateth the most remote regions in participation of their fruits, how much more are letters to be magnified, which, as ships, pass through the vast seas of time, and make ages so distant to participate of the wisdom, illuminations, and inventions, the one of the other?

Bacon, A, 90.

BOOKS are not absolutely dead things, but do contain a potency of life in them to be as active as that soul was whose progeny they are; nay, they do preserve as in a vial the purest efficacy and extraction of that living intellect that bred them.

Milton, I, 424.

THE chief glory of every people arises from its authors.
Dr. Johnson, W, IX, 227.

LXIII

AUTHORS

THERE has often been observed a manifest and striking contrariety between the life of an author and his writings. *Dr. Johnson, R*, No. 14.

To write, and to live, are very different. Many who praise virtue, do no more than praise it.

Ibid., W, III, 83.

FEW characters can bear the microscopic scrutiny of wit quickened by anger; and perhaps the best advice to authors would be, that they should keep out of the way of one another.

Ibid., 38.

THE reciprocal civility of authors is one of the most risible scenes in the farce of life.

Ibid., IV, 585.

To commence author is to claim praise.

Ibid., R, No. 93.

MODERN writers are the moons of literature; they shine with reflected light, with light borrowed from the ancients.

Ibid., B, III, 333.

No man loves to be indebted to his contemporaries.

Ibid., W, IV, 26.

THE promises of authors are like the vows of lovers.

Ibid., III, 82.

PRAISE is the tribute which every man is expected to pay for the grant of perusing a manuscript.

Ibid., M, II, 192.

THE man who is asked by an author what he thinks of his work, is put to the torture, and is not obliged to speak the truth.

Dr. Johnson, B, III, 320.

A MAN of genius has been seldom ruined but by himself.

Ibid., I, 381.

THE writer must live and die by his writing. Good for that, and good for nothing else.

Emerson, J, VII, 187.

GREAT men do not content us. . . . There is something indigent and tedious about them. They are poorly tied to one thought.

Ibid., E, III, 432.

ONE master could so easily be conceived as writing all the books of the world. They are all alike.

Ibid., J, VII, 297.

THE great writers were in their own age, as now, unique, . . . there is no such thing as a widely diffused level of high literary excellence.

Mackail, L, 85.

THE faults of great authors are generally excellencies carried to an excess.

Coleridge, M, 149.

No great work, or worthy of praise or memory, but came out of poor cradles.

Ben Jonson, 407.

OLD age is a good advertisement.

Emerson, J, X, 312.

LXIV

COMPOSITION

COMPOSITION is, for the most part, an effort of slow diligence and steady perseverance, to which the mind is dragged by necessity or resolution, and from which the attention is every moment starting to more delightful amusements.

Dr. Johnson, A, No. 138.

EVERY long work is lengthened by a thousand causes that can, and ten thousand that cannot, be recounted. Perhaps no extensive and multifarious performance was ever effected within the term originally fixed in the undertaker's mind. He that runs against time has an antagonist not subject to casualties.

Ibid., W, IV, 27.

A GREAT work, like a great house, was never yet finished at the given time.

Gibbon, M, I, 657.

WHAT is written without effort is in general read without pleasure.

Dr. Johnson, M, II, 309.

WHAT is easy is seldom excellent.

Ibid., W, IV, 134.

READY writing makes not good writing; but good writing brings on ready writing.

Ben Jonson, 411.

No precepts will profit a fool.

Ibid., 412.

THE more a man writes, the more he can write.

Hazlitt, D, 77.

HE who draws upon his own resources, easily comes to an end of his wealth.

Ibid., S A, 52.

DIFFICULTY is, for the most part, the daughter of idleness

Dr. Johnson, R, No. 129.

IT is best to throw life into a method, that every hour may bring its employment, and every employment have its hour.

Ibid., B, III, p. 94.

GREAT labour, directed by great abilities, is never wholly lost.

Ibid., W, II, 25.

SELF-CONFIDENCE is the first requisite to great undertakings.

Ibid., IV, 6.

A MAN may write at any time, if he will set himself doggedly to it.

Ibid., B, I, 203.

No great man will ever drill. None will ever solve the problem of his character according to our preconceived notions or wishes, but only in his own high, unprecedented way.

Emerson, J, V, 323.

IF your subject does not appear the flower of the world at this moment, you have not yet rightly got it.

Ibid., X, 174.

THE real essence of work is concentrated energy, . . . people who really have that in a superior degree by nature, are independent of the forms and habits and artifices by which less able and active people are kept up to their labours.

Bagehot, B, 370.

NOTHING is ended with honour which does not conclude better than it began.

Dr. Johnson, R, No. 207.

HE that is himself weary will soon weary the public
Ibid.

IT is a rule never to be forgotten, that whatever strikes strongly, should be described while the first impression remains fresh upon the mind

Ibid., B, I, 337.

THE style of an author should be the image of his mind, but the choice and command of language is the fruit of exercise.

Gibbon, M, I, 145.

A MAN's style is his mind's voice.

Emerson, J, X, 457.

THE rules of style, like those of law, arise from precedents often repeated.

Dr. Johnson, W, IX, 185.

THE only artists who can show great originality are those trained in distinct and established schools; for originality and genius must be largely fed and raised on the shoulders of some old tradition.

Santayana, R, II, 101.

I WILL like and praise some things in a young writer, which yet, if he continue in, I cannot but justly hate him for the same

Ben Jonson, 412.

SOME, for fear their orations should giggle, will not let them smile.

Thomas Fuller, H, 169.

EVERYTHING suffers by translation except a Bishop.

Chesterfield, 1271.

No man but a blockhead ever wrote, except for money.

Dr. Johnson, B, III, 19.

NECESSITY may be the mother of lucrative invention; but is the death of poetical.

Shenstone, 195.

As soon as any art is pursued with a view to money, then farewell, in ninety-nine cases out of a hundred, all hope of genuine good work.

Samuel Butler, N, 171.

IT is very hard to go beyond your public. If they are satisfied with your poor performance, you will not easily make it better

Emerson, J, IX, 304.

WHO would not like to write something which all can read, like Robinson Crusoe? And who does not see with regret that his page is not solid with a right materialistic treatment, which delights everybody?

Ibid., E, IV, 266.

226

COMPOSITION

THE longing to be primitive is a disease of culture; it is archaism in morals. To be so preoccupied with vitality is a symptom of anæmia.

Santayana, E, 163.

IF I were a Professor of English I would teach my men that prose writing is a kind of poetry.

Jowett, 249.

I SOMETIMES try to be miserable that I may do more work.

Blake, L, I, 163.

A MAN cannot say, "I will compose poetry." The greatest poet even cannot say it; for the mind in creation is as a fading coal, which some invisible influence, like an inconstant wind, awakens to transitory brightness.

Shelley, 41.

THE poet's habit of living should be set on a key so low that the common influences should delight him.

Emerson, E, I, 213.

No great work has ever been produced except after a long interval of still and musing meditation.

Bagehot, B, 112.

As man is now constituted, to be brief is almost a condition of being inspired

Santayana, E, 141.

LXV

READING

READING maketh a full Man; Conference a ready Man; and Writing an exact Man.

Bacon, E, 181.

THERE be some men are born only to suck out the poison of books.

Ben Jonson, 403.

PEOPLE in general do not willingly read, if they can have anything else to amuse them.

Dr. Johnson, B, IV, 218.

IT is strange that there should be so little reading in the world, and so much writing.

Ibid.

IF I do not read, nobody will.

Emerson, J, III, 460.

LET blockheads read what blockheads wrote.

Chesterfield, 364.

WHEN I am reading a book, whether wise or silly, it seems to me to be alive and talking to me.

Swift, XI, 322.

SOMETIMES I read a book with pleasure, and detest the author.

Ibid., 315.

OF all the artificial Relations, formed between Mankind, the most capricious and variable is that of Author and Reader.

Shaftesbury, III, 227.

READING

THERE are books . . . which take rank in our life with parents and lovers and passionate experiences.

Emerson, E, III, 100.

A MAN who has not read Homer is like a man who has not seen the ocean. There is a great object of which he has no idea.

Bagehot, L, I, 255.

I WISH only to read that which it would be a serious disaster to have missed.

Emerson, J, IX, 429.

WE read often with as much talent as we write.

Ibid., X, 67.

I SUPPOSE every old scholar has had the experience of reading something in a book which was significant to him, but which he could never find again. Sure he is that he read it there; but no one else ever read it, nor can he find it again, though he buy the book, and ransack every page.

Ibid., 204.

How attractive is the book in my friend's house which I should not read in my own!

Ibid., V, 37.

WHEN I read a good book . . . I wish that life were three thousand years long.

Ibid., X, 140.

LXVI

POETRY

THE gardens of the Muses keep the privilege of the Golden Age; they ever flourish and are in league with Time.

Bacon, L, I, 379.

POETRY is the record of the best and happiest moments of the happiest and best minds.

Shelley, 42.

A POET is a nightingale, who sits in darkness and sings to cheer its own solitude with sweet sounds.

Ibid., 14.

ADDICT not thyself to Poetry. Reputation is much oftener lost than gained by Verse.

Dr. Fuller, I, 25.

THE degree in which a poet's imagination dominates reality is, in the end, the exact measure of his importance and dignity.

Santayana, R, IV, 114.

POETS are the unacknowledged legislators of the World.

Shelley, 49.

POETRY should surprise by a fine excess, and not by singularity.

Keats, 77.

THE poet cannot descend into the turbid present without injury to his rarest gifts.

Emerson, E, IV, 175.

THERE is some reason to believe that, when a man does not write his poetry, it escapes by other vents through him, instead of the one vent of writing; clings to his form and manners, whilst poets have often nothing poetical about them except their verses.

Emerson, E, II, 292.

THE poet demands all gifts, and not one or two only.

Ibid., IV, 448.

Do not judge the poet's life to be sad because of his plaintive verses and confessions of despair. Because he was able to cast off his sorrows into these writings, therefore went he onward free and serene to new experiences.

Ibid., J, V, 520.

RHETORIC is either very good, or stark naught; there is no medium in rhetoric. If I am not fully persuaded, I laugh at the orator.

Selden, 109.

WHAT is so furious and Bethlem-like, as a vain sound of chosen and excellent words, without any subject of sentence and science mixed?

Ben Jonson, 394.

I HATE to see a load of band-boxes go along the street, and I hate to see a parcel of big words without anything in them.

Hazlitt, T T, II, 190.

To be bewitched is not to be saved, though all the magicians and æsthetes in the world should pronounce it to be so.

Santayana, R, IV, 167.

KNOWLEDGE of the subject is to the poet what durable materials are to the architect.

Dr. Johnson, W, II, 408.

WHATEVER can happen to man has happened so often that little remains for fancy or invention. We have been all born; we have most of us been married; and so many have died before us, that our deaths can supply but few materials for a poet.

Ibid., 389.

POETRY has not often been worse employed than in dignifying the amorous fury of a raving girl.

Ibid., W, IV, 15.

THEN, Sir, what is poetry?

Why, Sir, it is much easier to say what it is not. We all *know* what light is, but it is not easy to *tell* what it is.

Ibid., B, III, 38.

THE song of Comus has airiness and jollity; but, what may recommend Milton's morals as well as his poetry, the invitations to pleasure are so general, that they excite no distinct images of corrupt enjoyment, and take no dangerous hold on the fancy.

Ibid., W, II, 153.

ALL poetry is artificial, . . . the *Iliad* itself is artificial in a very eminent and unusual degree.

Mackail, L, 99.

EVERY poem must be made up of lines that are poems.

Emerson, J, VII, 523.

THE sweetest essences are always confined in the smallest glasses.

Dryden, II, 178.

TRAGEDY is the miniature of human life; an epic poem is the draught at length.

Dryden, II, 157.

'TIS one of the mysteries of our condition that the poet seems sometimes to have a mere talent,—a chamber in his brain into which an angel flies with divine messages, but the man, apart from this privilege, commonplace.

Emerson, J, X, 360.

POETS are not to be seen.

Ibid., 369.

ONLY write a dozen lines, and rest on your oars for ever.

Ibid., VII, 539.

A CROP of poets is as inevitable as a crop of violets or anemones.

Ibid., VII, 53

LXVII

FICTION

THERE is but one standard English novel, like the one orthodox sermon.

Emerson, E, IV, 170.

IT is curious how sleepy and foolish we are, that these tales will so take us. Again and again we have been caught in that old foolish trap:—then, as before, to feel indignant to have been duped and dragged after a foolish boy and girl, to see them at last married and portioned, and the reader instantly turned out of doors, like a beggar that has followed a gay procession into a castle.

Ibid.

How far off from life and manners and motives the novel still is! Life lies about us dumb; the day, as we know it, has not yet found a tongue.

Ibid., III, 114.

THE Peerage . . . is the best thing in fiction that the English have ever done.

Oscar Wilde, 60.

BIOGRAPHY, HISTORY

IF a man could say nothing against a character but what he can prove, history could not be written.

Dr. Johnson, B, III, 16.

MORE knowledge may be gained of a man's real character, by a short conversation with one of his servants, than from a formal and studied narrative, begun with his pedigree, and ended with his funeral.

Ibid., R, No. 60.

IF nothing but the bright side of characters should be shown, we should sit down in despondency, and think it utterly impossible to imitate them in anything.

Ibid., B, IV, 53.

ALL panegyrics are mingled with an infusion of poppy.

Swift, XI, 320.

SELDOM any splendid story is wholly true.

Dr. Johnson, W, II, 281.

HISTORIES of the downfall of kingdoms, and revolutions of empires, are read with great tranquillity.

Ibid., R, No. 60.

IN analysing history do not be too profound, for often the causes are quite superficial.

Emerson, J, IV, 160.

GOSSIP which is written down is no more veracious than gossip which flies current.

Bishop Creighton, MS.

GOSSIP is none the less gossip because it comes from venerable antiquity. *Ibid.*

ANYBODY can make history. Only a great man can write it. *Oscar Wilde,* 52.

CRITICISM

CRITICISM . . . is a serious and public function: it shows the race assimilating the individual, dividing the immortal from the mortal part of a soul.

Santayana, R, IV, 151.

WHILE an author is yet living, we estimate his powers by his worst performance; and when he is dead, we rate them by his best.

Dr. Johnson, W, IX, 240.

THERE is a certain race of men that either imagine it their duty, or make it their amusement, to hinder the reception of every work of learning or genius, who stand as sentinels in the avenues of fame, and value themselves upon giving Ignorance and Envy the first notice of a prey.

Ibid., R, No. 3.

THERE is nothing more dreadful to an author than neglect, compared with which reproach, hatred and opposition are names of happiness.

Ibid., No. 2.

IT is very rarely that an author is hurt by his critics.

Ibid., B, III, 423.

WHATEVER professes to benefit by pleasing, must please at once. The pleasures of the mind imply something sudden and unexpected; that which elevates must always surprise. *Ibid., W*, II, 65.

WHEN I take up the end of a web, and find it pack-thread, I do not expect, by looking further, to find embroidery. *Ibid., B*, II, 88.

HE who pleases many must have some species of merit.
Dr. Johnson, W, II, 279.

ABOUT things on which the public thinks long, it commonly attains to think right.
Ibid., III, 90.

THE thoughts of the best minds always become the last opinion of Society.
Emerson, L, I, 29.

THE best authority is the best argument; for generally to have pleased, and through all ages, must bear the force of universal tradition.
Dryden, I, 183.

THE French are as much better critics than the English as they are worse poets.
Ibid., II, 178.

WE do not say that a man to be a critic must necessarily be a poet: but to be a good critic, he ought not to be a bad poet.
Hazlitt, Sh, XVI.

IT is the business of reviewers to watch poets, not of poets to watch reviewers.
Ibid., E P, 296.

THERE is always an appeal open from criticism to nature.
Dr. Johnson, W, IX, 247.

LXX

TASTE

It is in rare and scattered instants that beauty smiles even on her adorers, who are reduced for habitual comfort to remembering her past favours

Santayana, E, 117.

If travellers were to describe the most laboured performances of art with the same coldness as they survey them, all expectations of happiness from change of place would cease. The pictures of Raphael would hang without spectators, and the gardens of Versailles might be inhabited by hermits.

Dr. Johnson, Idler, No. 50.

The perceptions as well as the senses may be improved to our own disquiet, and we may, by diligent cultivation of the powers of dislike, raise in time an artificial fastidiousness, which shall fill the imagination with phantoms of turpitude.

Ibid., R, No. 112.

It is the privilege only of deep reflection, or lively fancy, to destroy happiness by art and refinement.

Ibid.

There is no end of objections. There are few books to which some objection or other may not be made.

Ibid., B, III, 26.

Nowhere probably is there more true feeling, and nowhere worse taste, than in a churchyard.

Jowett, 244.

THERE is hardly a human life which would not have been different if the idea of beauty in the mind of the man who lived it had been different.

Bagehot, L, II, 431.

OPINION and affection extremely differ. . . . I love Apples the best of any fruit, it does not follow that I must think apples to be the best of fruit.

Selden, 87.

MEN lose their tempers in defending their taste.

Emerson, J, II, 147.

CULTURE is on the horns of this dilemma: if profound and noble it must remain rare, if common it must become mean.

Santayana, R, II, 111.

To have known the best, and to have known it for the best, is success in life.

Mackail, C, 207.

LXXI

ART

THERE is no excellent Beauty, that hath not some Strangeness in the Proportion.

Bacon, E, 156.

NOTHING but Nature can give a sincere pleasure; where that is not imitated, 'tis grotesque painting; the fine woman ends in a fish's tail.

Dryden, II, 161.

MEN at first produce effect by studying nature, and afterwards they look at nature only to produce effect.

Hazlitt, D, 139.

NOTHING is really so poor and melancholy as art that is interested in itself and not in its subject.

Santayana, R, IV, 152.

AN artist is a dreamer consenting to dream of the actual world.

Ibid., 39.

LIFE too near paralyses art.

Emerson, J, V, 292.

THE artists must be sacrificed to their art.   Like the bees, they must put their lives into the sting they give.

Ibid., E, III, 326.

EVERY artist was first an amateur.

Ibid., 300.

AN artist may visit a museum, but only a pedant can live there.

Santayana, R, IV, 129.

HE who can create works of art needs not collect them.
Emerson, E, III, 459.

A FOOL sees not the same tree that a wise man sees.
Blake.

EXUBERANCE is Beauty.
Ibid.

THE man who never in his mind and thought travelled
to heaven, is no artist.
Ibid., L, I, 310.

MERE enthusiasm is the all in all.
Ibid., 309.

PASSION and expression are beauty itself.
Ibid., 311.

EXECUTION is the Chariot of Genius.
Ibid.

NONE but blockheads copy one another.
Ibid., II, 174.

LET it no more be said that empires encourage arts,
for it is arts that encourage empires.   Arts and artist
are spiritual, and laugh at mortal contingencies.
Ibid., 173.

To admire on principle, is the only way to imitate
without loss of originality.
Coleridge, B, Chap. IV.

THE perfection of art is the destruction of art.
Hazlitt, A, II, 323.

THE history of art is the history of revivals.
Samuel Butler, N, 130.

THE sense of final inevitable decay humanizes, and gives an affecting character to the triumphs of exalted art. Imperishable works executed by perishable hands are a sort of insult to our nature, and almost a contradiction in terms. They are ungrateful children, and mock the makers.

Hazlitt, A, I, 43.

WHAT has reasoning to do with the art of painting?

Blake, L, I, 310.

To generalize is to be an idiot. *Ibid.*, 311.

I HAD rather see the portrait of a dog that I know than all the allegorical paintings they can show me in the world. *Dr. Johnson, B*, I, 364.

IT was once confessed to me, by a painter, that no professor of his art ever loved another.

Ibid., R, No. 64.

INDIFFERENT pictures, like dull people, must absolutely be moral.

Hazlitt, A, I, 16.

LANDSCAPE painting is the obvious resource of misanthropy. *Ibid.*, II, 233.

To build is to be robbed.

Dr. Johnson, Idler, No. 62.

A MUSICAL education is necessary for musical judgment. What most people relish is hardly music; it is rather a drowsy reverie relieved by nervous thrills.

Santayana, R, IV, 51.

MUSIC is essentially useless, as life is.

Ibid., E, 130.

LXXII

RELIGION

EVERY man, either to his terror or consolation, has some sense of religion.

Harrington, 484.

IDOLATRY is in a man's own thought, not in the opinion of another. *Selden*, 54.

A GREAT fear, when it is ill-managed, is the parent of superstition; but a discreet and well-guided fear produces religion.

Jeremy Taylor, L, 317.

I CAN hardly think there was ever any scared into Heaven.

Sir Thomas Browne, R, 112.

A MAN may be damned for despairing to be saved.

Jeremy Taylor, L, 259.

ONE demanding how God employed Himself before the world was made? had answer: that He was making hell for curious questioners.

Milton, I, 362.

SOME Negroes who believe the resurrection, think that they shall rise white.

Sir Thomas Browne, C, 64.

CASTING out devils is mere juggling; they never cast out any but what they first cast in.

Selden, 40.

THERE was never a merry world since the fairies left dancing, and the parson left conjuring.

Ibid., 91.

THE Clergy would have us believe them against our own reason, as the woman would have had her husband against his own eyes, when he took her with another man, which yet she stoutly denied: what, will you believe your own eyes before your own sweet wife?

Selden, 31.

THE Clergy in this Sense, of Divine Institution, that God hath made Mankind so weak that it must be deceived.

Halifax, 221.

IF the Clergy did not live like temporal Men, all the Power of Princes could not bring them under the temporal Jurisdiction.

Ibid., 220.

To a philosophic eye, the vices of the clergy are far less dangerous than their virtues.

Gibbon, H, xlix.

THE clergy are as like as peas. I cannot tell them apart.

Emerson, E, IV, 427.

To preach long, loud, and Damnation is the way to be cried up. We love a man that damns us and we run after him again to save us.

Selden, 39.

WHEN the imagination is continually led to the brink of vice by a system of terror and denunciations, people fling themselves over the precipice from the mere dread of falling.

Hazlitt, C, 57.

THE Tone in preaching does much in working upon the people's affections. If a man should make love in an ordinary tone, his Mistress would not regard him; and therefore he must whine. If a man should cry fire or Murder in an ordinary voice, nobody would come out to help him. *Selden,* 105.

MIRACLES are the swaddling-clothes of infant churches.
Thomas Fuller, C, II, 239.

THE Religion of one seems madness unto another.
Sir Thomas Browne, U, 20.

THE People would not believe in God at all, if they were not permitted to believe wrong in Him.
Halifax, 221.

THE several Sorts of Religion in the World are little more than so many spiritual Monopolies.

Ibid.

THE Papacy is no other than the Ghost of the deceased Roman Empire, sitting crowned upon the grave thereof.
Hobbes, 386.

DEFOE says that there were a hundred thousand stout country-fellows in his time ready to fight to the death against popery, without knowing whether popery was a man or a horse.

Hazlitt, S E, 101.

THE merit claimed for the Anglican Church is, that if you let it alone, it will let you alone.
Emerson, J, VIII, 368.

FACTIONS are like Pirates that set out false Colours; when they come near a Booty Religion is put under Deck.
Halifax, 221.

Most Men's Anger about Religion is as if two Men should quarrel for a Lady they neither of them care for.
Halifax, 221.

We have just enough religion to make us hate, but not enough to make us love one another.
Swift, III, 393.

You say you believe the Gospel: you live as if you were sure not one word of it is true.
Bishop Wilson, M, 44.

No man must go to heaven who has not sent his heart thither before.
Ibid., 66

Libertines fear nothing: the devils fear and tremble.
Ibid., 87.

Campbell is a good man, a pious man. I am afraid he has not been in the inside of a church for many years, but he never passes a church without pulling off his hat. This shows that he has good principles.
Dr. Johnson, B, I, 417.

Prisons are built with stones of Law, Brothels with bricks of Religion.
Blake.

So long as there are earnest believers in the world, they will always wish to punish opinions, even if their judgment tells them it is unwise, and their conscience that it is wrong.
Bagehot, L, II, 423.

The New Jerusalem, when it comes, will probably be found so far to resemble the old as to stone its prophets freely.
Samuel Butler, N, 175.

FANATICISM consists in redoubling your effort when you have forgotten your aim.

Santayana, R, I, 13.

PEOPLE are usually more firmly convinced that their opinions are precious than that they are true.

Ibid., V.

SCIENCE which thinks to make belief in miracles impossible is itself belief in miracles—in the miracles best authenticated by history and by daily life.

Ibid.

THE religions we call false were once true.

Emerson, E, IV, 314.

A SAINT is a sceptic once in twenty-four hours.

Ibid., J, VIII, 583.

'TIS incredible to us, if we look into the religious books of our grandfathers, how they held themselves in such a pinfold.

Ibid., E, IV, 316.

WE are born believing. A man bears beliefs, as a tree bears apples.

Ibid., II, 297.

THE brute necessity of believing something so long as life lasts does not justify any belief in particular.

Santayana, S, 9.

THE whole history of civilization is strewn with creeds and institutions which were invaluable at first, and deadly afterwards

Bagehot, P, 74.

THE religion of one age is the literary entertainment of the next.

Emerson, E, IV, 315

ARE you not scared by seeing that the Gypsies are more attractive to us than the Apostles?

Ibid., J, VI, 184.

OATHS are the fossils of piety.

Santayana, P, 148.

Do you believe in ghosts, Mr. Coleridge?
No, ma'am, I have seen too many.

Bagehot, B, 37.

THE Inquiry into a Dream is another Dream.

Halifax, 249.

MEN have feverishly conceived a heaven only to find it insipid, and a hell to find it ridiculous.

Santayana, E, 278.

MAN may rather be defined as a religious than a rational creature.

Harrington, 484.

STRONG beliefs win strong men, and then make them stronger.   *Bagehot, P, 76.*

WE must agree that in life itself intelligence is a superficial growth, and easily blighted, and that the experience of the vanity of the world, of sin, of salvation, of miracles, of strange revelations, and of mystic loves, is a far deeper, more primitive, and therefore probably more lasting human possession than is that of clear historical or scientific ideas.

Santayana, W, 56.

LXXIII

DEATH

I AM not so much afraid of death as ashamed thereof:
'tis the very disgrace and ignominy of our natures.

Sir Thomas Browne, R, 86.

DYING is something ghastly, as being born is something
ridiculous.

Santayana, E, 91.

A SUDDEN death is but a sudden joy, if it takes a man
in the state and exercises of virtue.

Jeremy Taylor, D, 154.

NEVER any weary traveller complained that he came
too soon to his journey's end.

Thomas Fuller, T, 24.

To smell to a turf of fresh earth is wholesome for the
body; no less are thoughts of mortality cordial to the
soul.

Ibid., H, 288.

WITH what shift and pains we come into the world,
we remember not; but 'tis found commonly no easy
matter to get out of it.

Sir Thomas Browne, C, 78.

WE are in the power of no calamity while death is in
our own.

Ibid., R, 95.

THE loss of our friends and companions impresses
hourly upon us the necessity of our own departure; we
know that the schemes of man are quickly at an end,
that we must soon lie down in the grave with the forgotten multitudes of former ages, and yield our place to

others, who, like us, shall be driven awhile by hope or fear, about the surface of the earth, and then like us be lost in the shades of death.

Dr. Johnson, R, No. 203.

THE death of great men is not always proportioned to the lustre of their lives. . . . The death of Pope was imputed by some of his friends to a silver saucepan, in which it was his delight to heat potted lampreys.

Ibid., W, IV, 92.

I HAVE heard it remarked by a statesman of high reputation, that most great men have died of over-eating themselves.

Sir Henry Taylor, S, 230.

THE long habit of living indisposeth us for dying.

Sir Thomas Browne, U, 25.

THE sense of security more frequently springs from habit than from conviction. . . . The older a man gets, the more difficult it is for him to retain a believing conception in his own death.

George Eliot, Silas Marner.

To himself every one is an immortal; he may know that he is going to die, but he can never know that he is dead.

Samuel Butler, N, 357.

OUR dead are never dead to us until we have forgotten them; they can be injured by us, they can be wounded.

George Eliot, Adam Bede.

THOSE who have endeavoured to teach us to die well, have taught few to die willingly.

Dr. Johnson, B, I, 365.

BUT is not the fear of death natural to man?

So much so, Sir, that the whole of life is but keeping away the thoughts of it.　　　*Dr. Johnson, B*, II, 93.

AFTER a certain distance, every step we take in life we find the ice growing thinner below our feet, and all around us and behind us we see our contemporaries going through.

　　　　　　　　R. L. Stevenson, V, 157.

PERSONS are not wanting, apparently free from ecclesiastical constraint, who still maintain that the value of life depends on its indefinite prolongation.

　　　　　　　　Santayana, E, 97.

WE do not die wholly at our deaths: we have mouldered away gradually long before. . . . Death only consigns the last fragment of what we were to the grave.

　　　　　　　　Hazlitt, WS, 76.

TYRAWLEY and I have been dead these two years; but we don't choose to have it known.

　　　　　　　　Chesterfield.

ALL I desire for my own burial is not to be buried alive; but how or where, I think, must be entirely indifferent to every rational creature.

　　　　　　　　Ibid., 1383.

ULYSSES in *Hecuba* cared not how meanly he lived, if he might find a noble Tomb after death.

　　　　　Sir Thomas Browne, U, 11.

IN taking away our friends, death does not take them away utterly, but leaves behind a mocking, tragical, and soon intolerable residue, which must be hurriedly concealed.　　　*R. L. Stevenson, V*, 153.

WHEN we attend a funeral, we are apt to comfort ourselves with the happy difference that is betwixt us and our dead friend.

Bishop Wilson, M, 34.

WORLDLY faces never look so worldly as at a funeral.
George Eliot, Janet's Repentance.

IF a man will observe as he walks the streets, I believe he will find the merriest countenances in mourning-coaches.

Swift, III, 400.

THE difficulty in writing epitaphs is to give a particular and appropriate praise. This, however, is not always to be performed, whatever be the diligence or ability of the writer; for the greater part of mankind *have no character at all*, have little that distinguishes them from others equally good or bad, and therefore nothing can be said of them which may not be applied with equal propriety to a thousand more. It is indeed no great panegyric, that there is enclosed in this tomb one who was born in one year, and died in another; yet many useful and amiable lives have been spent which yet leave little materials for any other memorial.

Dr. Johnson, W, IV, 151.

OUT of doors, in the snow, in the fields, death looks not funereal, but natural, elemental, even fair. Indoors it looks disagreeable.

Emerson, J, V, 482.

DRIVE your cart and your plow over the bones of the dead. *Blake.*

ENOUGH! or Too much. *Ibid.*

LIST OF AUTHORS AND WORKS QUOTED

ARNOLD, Matthew, 1822–1888:
    Essays in Criticism. 3rd ed., 1875.

BACON, Francis, 1561–1626:
    A. Of the Proficience and Advancement of Learning.
        Edited by G. W. Kitchin, M.A. 1861.
    E. Essays by Francis Lord Verulam. Edited by B.
        Montagu. 1845.
BAGEHOT, Walter, 1826–1877:
    B. Biographical Studies. 1914.
    E. The English Constitution. 1867.
    L. Literary Studies. 2 vols., 4th ed., 1891.
    P. Physics and Politics. N.D.
BERKELEY, George, 1685–1753. Bishop of Cloyne:
    Commonplace Books. Works, 1901. Vol. I.
BLAKE, William, 1757–1827:
    L. Life of William Blake, by Alexander Gilchrist.
        2 vols., 2nd ed., 1880.
    The other quotations from Blake are from "The
    Marriage of Heaven and Hell."
BRADLEY, F. H.:
    Appearance and Reality. 1920.
BROWNE, Sir Thomas, 1605–1682:
    C. Christian Morals. 2nd ed., 1756.
    R. Religio Medici. 4th ed., 1656.
    U. Hydriotaphia Urne-Buriall. 1658. Printed in
        the following—
    V. Pseudodoxia Epidemica: or, Enquiries into Very
        Many Received Tenets. 4th ed., 1658.
BUTLER, Samuel, 1612–1680:
    The Genuine Remains in Verse and Prose of Mr.
    Samuel Butler, author of "Hudibras." 1759. Vol.
    II.
BUTLER, Samuel, 1835–1902:
    E. Collected Essays. 1925. Vol. II.

N. The Note-Books of Samuel Butler. 1919.
W. The Way of All Flesh. 1922.

CARLISLE, Countess Dowager of:
> Thoughts in the form of Maxims: addressed to Young Ladies on their Establishment in the World. 2nd ed., 1790.

CHESTERFIELD, Philip Dormer Stanhope, fourth Earl of, 1694–1773:
> *W.* Miscellaneous Works, edited by M. Maty. 4 vols., 1777–9.
> The other Chesterfield quotations are from "The Letters of Lord Chesterfield," edited by John Bradshaw. 1892.

COLERIDGE, Samuel Taylor, 1772–1834:
> *A.* Anima Poetæ. 1895.
> *B.* Biographia Literaria.
> *M.* Miscellanies. 1911.
> *T T.* Table Talk and Omniana. 1917.

COLLINS, John Churton, 1848–1908:
> *E.* Aphorisms in the "English Review," April, 1914.
> *L.* Life and Memoirs of John Churton Collins, by L. C. Collins. 1912.

CREIGHTON, Mandell, 1843–1901, Bishop of London.
> *L.* Life and Letters, by L. Creighton. 2 vols., 1904.
> *MS.* Manuscript Notes.

DONNE, John, 1573–1631:
> LXXX Sermons. 1640.

DRYDEN, John, 1631–1700:
> Essays of John Dryden. Selected and edited by W. P. Ker. 2 vols., 1900.

EMERSON, Ralph Waldo, 1803–1882:
> *E.* The Works of Ralph Waldo Emerson. 5 vols., 1913.

J. Journals of Ralph Waldo Emerson. 10 vols., 1910–1914.

L. The Correspondence of Thomas Carlyle and Ralph Waldo Emerson. 2 vols., 1883.

FULLER, Thomas, D.D., 1608–1661:
C. The Church History of Britain. 3 vols., 1837.
H. The Holy State, and the Profane State. With Notes by James Nichols. 1841.
P. A Pisgah Sight of Palestine. 1869.
T. Good Thoughts in Bad Times: Good Thoughts in Worse Times: Mixed Contemplations in Better Times. 1830.
W. The History of the Worthies of England, edited by John Nichols. 1811.

FULLER, Dr. Thomas, 1654–1734:
Introductio ad Prudentiam; or, Directions, Counsels, and Cautions, tending to a Prudent Management of Affairs in Common Life. Vol. I, 3rd ed., 1731. Vol. II, 2nd ed., 1740.

GIBBON, Edward, 1737–1794:
H. The History of the Decline and Fall of the Roman Empire.
M. Miscellaneous Works. 2 vols., 1796.

HALIFAX, Lord, 1633–1695:
The complete Works of George Savile, first Marquess of Halifax, edited by Walter Raleigh. 1912.

HARRINGTON, James, 1611–1677:
The Oceana and other Works of James Harrington, edited by John Toland. 1771.

HAZLITT, William, 1778–1830:
A. Criticisms on Art. 2 vols., 1843.
B. The Life of Napoleon Buonaparte. 4 vols., 1830.
C. Characteristics: in the Manner of Rochefoucault's Maxims. 1823.

D.   Lectures chiefly on the Dramatic Literature of the Age of Elizabeth. 1820.

E C.   Lectures on the English Comic Writers. 1819.

E P.   Lectures on the English Poets. 1818.

J.   Notes of a Journey through France and Italy. 1826.

L R.   Literary Remains. 2 vols., 1836.

N.   Conversations of James Northcote, R.A. 1830.

P E.   Political Essays. 1819.

P P.   Parliamentary Portraits. 1815.

P S.   The Plain Speaker. 2 vols., 1826.

R T.   The Round Table. 2 vols., 1817.

S A.   The Spirit of the Age. 1825.

S E.   Sketches and Essays. 1839.

Sh.   Characters of Shakspear's Plays. 1817.

T T.   Table Talk. 2 vols., 2nd ed., 1824.

W.   Collected Works. 12 vols., 1904.

W S.   Winterslow. 1850.

HOBBES, Thomas, 1588–1679:

     Leviathan. 1651.

JOHNSON, Samuel, 1709–1784:

A.   The Adventurer.

B.   Boswell's Life of Johnson, edited by George Birkbeck Hill. 6 vols., 1887.

H.   Wit and Wisdom of Samuel Johnson. 1888.

Idler.   The Idler.

L.   Letters of Samuel Johnson. Collected and edited by George Birkbeck Hill. 2 vols., 1892.

M.   Johnsonian Miscellanies. Arranged and edited by George Birkbeck Hill. 1897.

R.   The Rambler.

W.   Works of Samuel Johnson, LL.D., edited by Sir John Hawkins. 1787.

JONSON, Ben, 1573?–1637:

     The Works of Ben Jonson, edited by Francis Cunningham. 1897. Vol. III.

JOWETT, Benjamin, 1817–1893:
  Letters of Benjamin Jowett, M.A. 1899.

KEATS, John, 1795–1821:
  Letters of John Keats, edited by Sidney Colvin. 1891.

MACKAIL, J. W.:
  C. Classical Studies. 1925.
  L. Latin Literature. 1895.
MILTON, John, 1608–1674.
  A Complete Collection of the Historical, Political, and
    Miscellaneous Works of John Milton. 3 vols., 1698.

PATMORE, Coventry, 1823–1896:
  Memoirs and Correspondence of Coventry Patmore,
    by Basil Champneys. 1900. Vol. II.
PENN, William, 1644–1718:
  Some Fruits of Solitude by William Penn, with an
    Introduction by Edmund Gosse. 1900.
POPE, Alexander, 1688–1744:
  Thoughts on Various Subjects, in Swift's "Works."
    1754. Vol. IV.

SANTAYANA, George:
  E. Little Essays drawn from the Writings of George
        Santayana. 1920.
  P. Interpretations of Poetry and Religion. 1916.
  R. The Life of Reason. 5 vols., 1914.
  S. Scepticism and Animal Faith. 1923.
  V. Various Articles and Essays.
  W. Words of Doctrine. 1913.
SELDEN, John, 1584–1654:
  Table Talk of John Selden, newly edited by Sir
    Frederick Pollock, Bt. 1927.
SHAFTESBURY, Anthony Ashley Cooper, 3rd Earl of, 1671–
    1713.
  Characteristicks of Men, Manners, Opinions, Times.
    3 vols., 5th ed., 1732.

SHAW, George Bernard:
>   Maxims for Revolutionists, in Man and Superman.
>   1903.
SHELLEY, Percy Bysshe, 1792–1822:
>   Essays, Letters from Abroad. 1852. Vol. I.
SHENSTONE, William, 1714–1763:
>   Essays on Men, Manners, and Things. Works, 1764,
>   Vol. II.
STEVENSON, Robert Louis, 1850–1894:
>   *B.* Familiar Studies of Men and Books. 6th ed.,
>   1891.
>   *E.* Ethical Studies. Works, Tusitala edition, 1924.
>   *M.* Memories and Portraits. 2nd ed., 1888.
>   *V.* Virginibus Puerisque. 6th ed., 1891.
SWIFT, Jonathan, 1667–1745:
>   The Works of Dr. Jonathan Swift. 12 vols., 1754–5.

TAYLOR, Sir Henry, 1800–1886:
>   *N.* Notes from Life in Six Essays. 3rd ed., 1849.
>   *S.* The Statesman. 1836.
TAYLOR, Jeremy, 1613–1667:
>   *D.* The Rule and Exercises of Holy Dying. 1651.
>   *L.* The Rule and Exercises of Holy Living. 4th
>   ed., 1654.
>   *S.* I. A Course of Sermons. 1653. II. XXVIII
>   Sermons. 1651.
THACKERAY, William Makepeace, 1811–1863:
>   Roundabout Papers. Works, 1877. Vol. X.

WILDE, Oscar, 1856–1900:
>   Aphorisms of Oscar Wilde. 4th ed., 1923.
WILSON, Thomas, 1663–1755, Bishop of Sodor and Man:
>   *M.* Maxims of Piety and of Christianity. 1898.
>   *S.* Sacra Privata. Works, 1860. Vol. V.

INDEX

INDEX

INDEX

Printed in Great Britain by Butler & Tanner Ltd., Frome and London